SCHOLASTIC

Traits Writing™

Student Handbook

Credits

Cover: © David Young-Wolff/PhotoEdit Inc.; p. 39 b: © Kenneth Garrett/National Geographic Stock;
p. 47 b: © David Young-Wolff/PhotoEdit Inc.; p. 55 b: © Gabriele Tamborrelli/iStockphoto; p. 65 b: © Trista Weibell/
iStockphoto; p. 73 b: © Ian Holland/Shutterstock; p. 81 b: © Randy Faris/Corbis/Glow Images; c: © Scholastic,
Inc.; p. 91 b: © PavelSh/Shutterstock; p. 99 b: © Robert Michael/Corbis/Glow Images; p. 107 b: © Regien Paassen/
Shutterstock; p. 117 b: © Elena Schweitzer/iStockphoto; p. 125 b: © Eyal Nahmias/Alamy; p. 133 b: © Andrey
Armyagov/Shutterstock; p. 143 b: © Chris Whitehead/Jupiterimages; p. 151 b: © dbimages/Alamy; p. 159 b: © Steven
Bourelle/Thinkstock; p. 169 b: © Marema/Shutterstock; p. 177 b: © Benjamin Albiach Galan/Shutterstock;
p. 185 b: © Emily Teresa; p. 195 b: © Dmitry Rukhlenko/Shutterstock; p. 203 b: © Terry Wild Stock Photography;
p. 211 b: © David Young Wolff/PhotoEdit Inc.

Trait Mates Illustrations: Wook Jin Jung

Contents

Week

1

The Writing Process

Week

2

Prewriting

Week

3

Drafting

Week

4

Revising

Week

5

Editing

Getting Started

The writing process helps you understand how to create a piece of writing. The writing traits give you a common language for discussing and assessing what you create. The traits are

- Ideas
- Organization
- Voice
- Word Choice
- Sentence Fluency
- Conventions
- Presentation

In the weeks to come, you'll learn more about each trait and how to use it as you prewrite, draft, revise, edit, and publish your writing. What makes the traits so great? They help YOU become a great writer!

Steps in the Writing Process

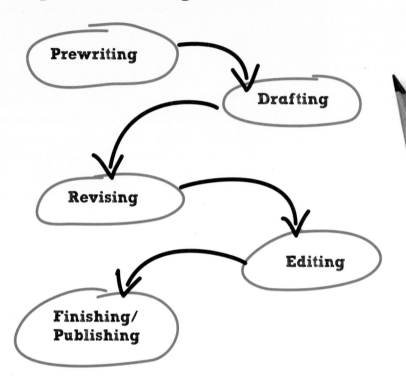

The Writing Process

Prewriting, drafting, revising, editing, and finishing and publishing are steps in the writing process. As you work through these steps, you share your writing with others and strive to improve it. That's where the writing traits come in. The traits help you know what to do at each step of the writing process. As a result, your writing gets stronger and stronger.

The Writing Process

Prewriting

- Use prewriting techniques such as brainstorming and generating questions to gather information.
- Think about the best way to organize your thoughts.
- Consider your audience and your purpose for writing.

Drafting

- Use prewriting ideas to make drafting decisions.
- Let ideas flow, knowing you can revise later on.
- Get thoughts down without worrying too much about conventions.
- Begin to structure the body.

Revising

- Use accurate and interesting details that reveal your unique perspective on the topic.
- Establish a tone that will connect with the reader.
- Start out strong and end just as strong.
- Refine words and sentences so they are precise and varied.

Editing

- Check spelling and look up words, if needed.
- Punctuate sentences accurately and start paragraphs in the right places.
- Use capital letters correctly.
- Apply standard rules of English grammar.

The last step in the writing process is actually "dancing," but we like to keep that a secret.

Taylor Mali on the Writing Process and the Traits

Group Members:

_____

Stanza:

_____

_____

_____

_____

_____

References to the Writing Process:

_____

_____

_____

_____

References to the Traits:

_____

_____

_____

_____

Trait Smart Presentation

Fill out this sheet to plan your trait presentation.

Trait: _____

Definition: _____

Write three similes or metaphors about the trait that reveal an important aspect of it. For example, you might write, "Sentence Fluency is like a river—writing should flow smoothly, yet at different speeds at different points along the way." For inspiration, check the trait's icon and the week opener photographs in this handbook.

1. _____

_____

2. _____

_____

3. _____

_____

Summarize your thoughts about the trait and its importance to writing.

_____

_____

_____

_____

_____

_____

The Writing Process

Ye Olde Traits

Meriwether Lewis learned a lot about writing from President Thomas Jefferson. Read the list of qualities of his writing that improved, according to the excerpt from *Undaunted Courage*. Then write each quality beside the trait to which it most closely relates.

Sense of Pace	Similes and Analogies
Timing	Descriptive Powers
Word Choice	Ability to "Catch a Reader Up"
Rhythm	Emotions Expressed Naturally and Effectively
Flow of Narrative	Sentences That Cry Out for Punctuation
The Precise Phrase	Personal Observations and Reactions

Ideas	
Organization	
Voice	
Word Choice	
Sentence Fluency	
Conventions	
Presentation	

Mode Mix-Up

Choose a book you like that contains passages written in the three modes:

Narrative (to tell a story)

Expository (to inform or explain)

Persuasive (to construct an argument)

Title: _____

Author: _____

Primary Mode: _____

Select three passages from the book that represent each mode well, bookmark them, and fill in the information below.

Passage #1

page number: _____ mode: _____

Passage #2

page number: _____ mode: _____

Passage #3

page number: _____ mode: _____

Now read the passages to members of another group and have them identify the mode in which it was written. Talk about why the passage is a good example of that mode.

Steps in the Writing Process

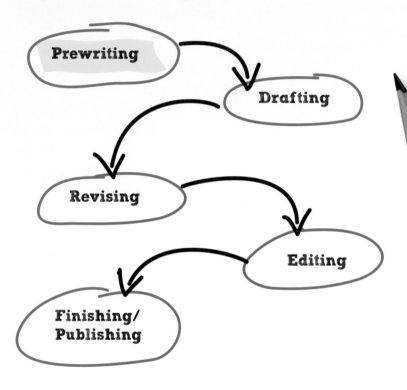

Prewriting → Drafting → Revising → Editing → Finishing/ Publishing

Prewriting

When you prewrite, you choose a topic for writing, identify your purpose and audience, and begin to organize what you will say and how you will say it. Prewriting is essential because it helps you explore writing possibilities and gives you a place to begin.

[Think About: **Prewriting**]

☐ Did I outline my main points, read a Web article or listen to a podcast, record ideas in my journal, interview an expert, observe the world with a writer's eyes and ears, create storyboards to capture scenes, and/or draw or freewrite different ideas about my topic?

☐ Did I think through my topic so it is clear and focused?

☐ Did I plan the best way to organize my ideas?

☐ Did I consider the audience for my writing and choose a voice that will speak to that audience?

> Do you have enough periods, commas, and question marks handy?

> Cool it, Conventions. You'll get your turn!

Conventions

Ideas

Prewriting for All Seasons

My <u>favorite </u>season of the year:

winter   spring   summer   fall

A day of the week during that season that is special to me:

_____

What makes it special:

_____

_____

_____

The best hour of that day for a special activity:

_____

What's so great about this activity?

_____

_____

_____

In the space below or on a separate sheet of paper, write a description of your activity that's so vivid the reader will know exactly why you chose it.

Tracking Down the Traits

Plan your group presentation about the trait you were assigned.

My Group's Trait: _____

Definition of the Trait (in your own words): _____

_____

_____

The Trait's Key Qualities:

1. _____

2. _____

3. _____

4. _____

Read the student-written passages on the Trait Passages sheet, assign a key quality to each one, and explain why you chose it.

Passage 1: _____

_____

Passage 2: _____

_____

Passage 3: _____

_____

Passage 4: _____

_____

Write From Experience

List some ideas for writing, inspired by events in your own life or things you have observed in the world. After each idea, identify the purpose of the piece and the mode in which you'd write it:

- to tell a story (narrative)
- to inform or explain (expository)
- to construct an argument (persuasive)

1. _____

_____

_____

Purpose and Mode: _____

2. _____

_____

_____

Purpose and Mode: _____

3. _____

_____

_____

Purpose and Mode: _____

Circle the idea you find most interesting. On a separate sheet of paper, apply a prewriting technique to arrive at a more focused topic. Then, write your topic here.

Focused Topic: _____

Two Great Traits

Work with a partner to identify the two writing traits you think Gary Soto applied most skillfully in the passage from *Taking Sides*. Write each trait below and give examples from the passage that support your response.

1. Trait: _____

▶ Examples from passage:

_____

_____

_____

_____

_____

2. Trait: _____

▶ Examples from passage:

_____

_____

_____

_____

_____

Share your responses with another pair of classmates. Be sure to have solid reasons for your choices, using language from the Student-Friendly Scoring Guides.

Steps in the Writing Process

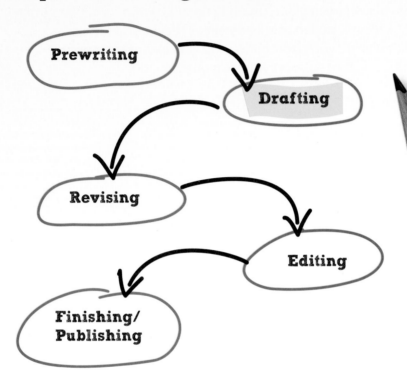

Prewriting → Drafting → Revising → Editing → Finishing/Publishing

Drafting

When you prewrite, you come up with a topic for a piece and begin to think about organization and voice. When you draft, you fine-tune your thinking even further by considering why you're writing the piece and who will read it. You might think about your lead, your ending, and details to include in the body. A rough draft should be just that: rough. You'll polish the piece when you revise. For now, you just need to get the piece moving.

[Think About: **Drafting**]

☐ Did I refer to my prewriting ideas before starting to write?

☐ Did I let my ideas flow, knowing I can add, cut, or change anything I want to later on?

☐ Did I think about what the reader might want or need to know about my topic?

☐ Am I moving toward a strong beginning, middle, and end in a way that is easy to follow?

☐ Did I get my ideas down without worrying too much about spelling, punctuation, capitalization, and grammar?

Just letting ideas flow . . . not worrying about spelling and stuff . . . getting out what's in my brain . . . putting it on paper . . . sorting it out . . .

He's on a roll. I'm totally getting out of his way.

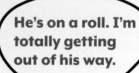

On Drafting

"Almost all good writing begins with terrible first efforts."
—Anne Lamott

"The scariest moment is always just before you start."
—Stephen King

Based on what they say here, what advice do you think these writers would have about drafting?

Anne Lamott:

_____

_____

_____

_____

Stephen King:

_____

_____

_____

_____

What do <u>YOU</u> think is most important to keep in mind as you draft?

_____

_____

_____

_____

Announce This!

Write a draft of a typical announcement you hear on your school's public-address system.

_____

_____

_____

_____

_____

Now think of a way to say it to make it much more interesting, so that your schoolmates will really pay attention.

What voice(s) do you think will work best?

___ frustrated   ___ irritating

___ silly   ___ nasty

___ thoughtful   ___ bold

___ witty   ___ melancholy

___ other _____

Draft your new announcement here. Connect to the audience!

_____

_____

_____

_____

_____

_____

Drafting

Assessing the Mentor Text

Using the Student-Friendly Scoring Guide for the trait you
selected, assess the passage from *Click* by Linda Sue Park.

Trait _____   **Score** _____

Provide two examples from the passage that justify your score.

1. _____

   _____

   _____

2. _____

   _____

   _____

Record the final scores for each trait here.

Ideas	Organization	Voice	Word Choice	Sentence Fluency

Adding On

Expand on Gee's story from *Click* by choosing an object other than a photo and drafting the story behind it. When you finish, read your piece to a partner and discuss the traits you applied particularly well.

_____

_____

_____

_____

_____

_____

_____

_____

_____

_____

_____

_____

_____

What did you learn about drafting from this activity?

_____

_____

_____

Steps in the Writing Process

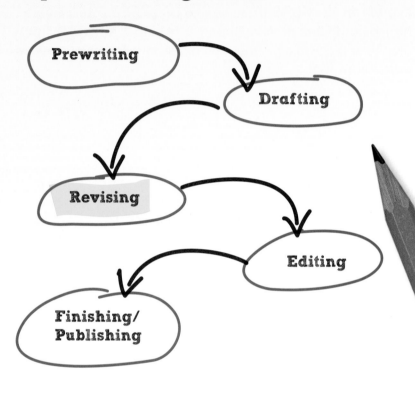

Prewriting → Drafting → Revising → Editing → Finishing/Publishing

Revising

You discover what you want to say when you prewrite and get your ideas down on paper when you draft. From there, you revise. You add, delete, reword, and rearrange material to make your writing strong and clear. Revising can be challenging, but the traits make it easier by giving you something concrete to think about. Even the most accomplished writers revise. Once the piece says exactly what they want it to, they move on to editing.

Think About: **Revising**

☐ Did I use accurate and original details to elaborate on the main idea?

☐ Do all the parts of the piece fit together logically from beginning to end?

☐ Did I add energy to the piece by expressing how I think and feel about the topic?

☐ Are my words and sentences precise, fresh, and varied?

Life as a Screenwriter

Mike Rich is a screenwriter—and it is a fascinating job. Like novelists, screenwriters write stories. Unlike novelists, they get to see their stories played out on the big screen. That's the fun part. What's not so fun are the revisions to their screenplays that directors often request on short notice. It's not easy work, but it's satisfying.

1. What advice do you think a screenwriter would offer to help you become a better writer?

    _____

    _____

    _____

2. Which step in the writing process do you think is the most challenging for a screenwriter? Why?

    _____

    _____

    _____

Talk with your partner after hearing Mike Rich's thoughts on being a screenwriter. Jot down any new ideas or insights you heard.

_____

_____

_____

_____

Revision All Around

Think about how your writing changes when you revise it. Then, think about and write down how the things below might change when you revise them.

➤ **A Recipe**

_____

_____

➤ **A Painting**

_____

_____

➤ **A Building Plan**

_____

_____

➤ **A Hairstyle**

_____

_____

➤ **A Video Game Concept**

_____

_____

➤ **A Feeling**

_____

_____

Revising

Game Time

Put a new spin on an old game. Go online to find a description of a game of your choice. Then revise the description. Your goal: To make a whole new generation of kids want to play the game! Include the following information:

- the name of the game
- the object of the game
- a brief overview of how the game is played
- the number of players or teams
- the components, such as a board, pieces, dice, and cards
- . . . and, most important, what makes the game fun to play

Who suggested "Pin the Tail on the Puzzle Piece"? That's not funny!

Ideas

Write your game description here.

Game: _____

_____

_____

_____

_____

_____

_____

_____

_____

_____

_____

Eye-Catching Packaging

Design the packaging for the game you chose. Start by writing the copy that will appear on the box, based on the game description you wrote earlier in the week.

_____

_____

_____

_____

_____

_____

_____

Next, sketch the box. Show how your copy will fit and flow. Then create a final version on chart paper or poster board.

Steps in the Writing Process

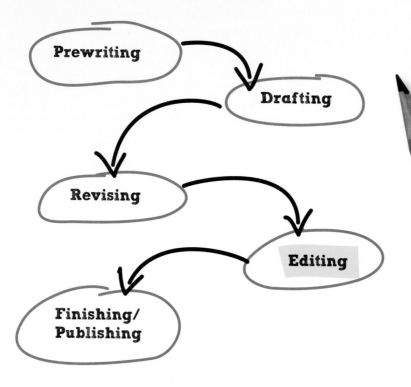

Prewriting → Drafting → Revising → Editing → Finishing/Publishing

Editing

After you prewrite, draft, and revise your piece, it's time to edit it, or clean it up for the reader. This is an important step in the writing process because, for the reader to understand what you have to say, he or she can't be confused by errors in spelling, punctuation, paragraphing, capitalization, or grammar and usage. When you edit, you apply rules of standard English to make sure your piece is a breeze to read and easy to understand.

Think About: **Editing**

- ☐ Did I check my spelling against a print or electronic resource and, if necessary, correct any misspelled words?

- ☐ Did I use punctuation accurately and effectively to make my ideas flow?

- ☐ Did I start paragraphs in the right places?

- ☐ Did I capitalize words correctly?

- ☐ Did I follow the rules of standard English grammar and usage? Or did I break them for stylistic reasons?

A whole section devoted to editing? NOW we're talking!

Conventions

Don't get carried away. Sit back and relax a spell.

Presentation

I Think I Know What You Mean

Edit six of the sentences on the Student Writing Bloopers sheet.
Spell the words the way the writers intended them to be spelled.
Save the writers from embarrassment!

1. _____

_____

_____

2. _____

_____

_____

3. _____

_____

_____

4. _____

_____

_____

5. _____

_____

_____

6. _____

_____

_____

"No Excuses" Agreement

Six rules of standard English that I will follow every time I write—without being reminded.

1. _____

   _____

2. _____

   _____

3. _____

   _____

4. _____

   _____

5. _____

   _____

6. _____

   _____

I agree to check my writing against this list whenever I'm taking it to completion. I am my own best editor!

_____

Signature

Conventions Collection

Look through mentor texts, books, magazines, and websites to find examples of conventions applied well. Find two good examples for each one, including examples that show how conventions can be used creatively, for impact.

Pssst . . . Wanna buy some conventions? I've got plenty, and I'll sell 'em cheap . . . really cheap.

Spelling

1. _____

2. _____

Source(s): _____

Punctuation

1. _____

2. _____

Source(s): _____

Capitalization

1. _____

2. _____

Source(s): _____

Grammar and Usage

1. _____

2. _____

Source(s): _____

Position Statement Planner

Brainstorm possible topics for your position statement, focusing on the theme of responsibility. After each topic, write down the stand, or position, you plan to take.

1. Topic: _____
   My stand on it:

   _____

   _____

2. Topic: _____
   My stand on it:

   _____

   _____

3. Topic: _____
   My stand on it:

   _____

   _____

My position paper will be about: _____

I chose this topic because: _____

_____

_____

_____

_____

Editing

Editing Marks

Mark	Meaning	Example
℘	Delete material.	The writing is is good.
sp	Correct the spelling or spell it out.	We are exploring ② traits this weak.
◯	Close space.	To day is publishing day.
∧	Insert a letter, word, or phrase.	My teacher has books. wonderful
℘	Change a letter.	She is a great wroter. i
⧣	Add a space.	Don't forget astrong lead.
∿	Transpose letters or words.	She raed the piece with flair!
≡	Change to a capital letter.	We have j. k. Rowling to thank for Harry Potter's magic.
/	Change to a lowercase letter.	"A Writer's work is never Done" was his favorite saying.
¶	Start a new paragraph.	"What day is it?" he inquired. ¶ "It's National Writing Day," she replied.
⊙	Add a period.	Think about all the traits as you write ⊙

UNIT 2

Focus Mode: Persuasive

If you want to be heard, it's important to know how to construct an argument. When you write in the persuasive mode, you write to convince the reader to agree with—or at least respect—your opinion on an important topic. You should clearly state your topic and position at the beginning and from there, defend your position, using solid facts, irrefutable evidence, and a confident tone.

- **Finding a Topic** ····················
- Focusing the Topic
- Developing the Topic
- Using Details

Focus Mode: Persuasive
Theme: Responsibility

Ideas

Ideas are your central message—the main thoughts you want to share. To make your ideas strong, choose a topic you care about and focus on one interesting aspect of it. From there, weave in original and unexpected details to open your readers' eyes and show them something they might otherwise overlook.

Finding a Topic

Last time I cleaned my bedroom, I unearthed an ancient peanut-butter-and-jelly sandwich.

Topics for writing are all around you—in what you see, hear, experience, and daydream about every day. When you find the perfect topic, your mind races with exciting possibilities. Your main objective should be to offer a clear, central theme or simple, original story line—something unique, important, meaningful, and memorable.

Ideas

How is finding a topic like going on an archaeological dig?

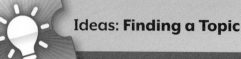

Ideas in Unusual Places

You probably already know the usual places to find ideas for writing—your life, your hopes and dreams, your friends, school, family memories, special events, and your hobbies and interests. Here are some other places to explore. Notice how each example can be written in any mode.

Special Interest Magazines

Surfboarding, hair or fashion design, home repair, social networking and technology—there are magazines for almost every interest out there.

Example: trading card collectors magazine

- narrative—sci-fi story about nanocards that can control natural resources
- expository—sports photographers who have captured award-winning shots

Photographs

Check out old family photographs or pictures of people and places online. Imagine what they might be thinking and why, or what could happen there.

Example: photos of the rain forest

- narrative—girl with a troubled past finds her way working at a nature center
- persuasive—piece on why it's important to preserve the rain forests

Song Lyrics

Music can make you feel a certain way or evoke memories. The mood of a song can make you think of scenic surroundings, or of someone in particular.

Example: ballad about a first crush

- narrative—story of something embarrassing that happened in front of a crush
- expository—directions for a love potion; 10 Ways to Live a Fulfilling Single Life
- persuasive—petition to limit the number of pop songs per year about crushes

News Sources

You might be deeply passionate about something—and not even know it! Hidden in newspapers and magazines, radio, television, and online news lie topics that might inspire you to write a striking piece.

Example: news story about a town that was washed away in a flood

- expository—list of buildings destroyed, and their historical significance
- persuasive—speech or poster about the dangers of deforestation

What are some other unusual places to find ideas? Record them here.

_____

R.A.F.T.S. 1

You are the special-events manager at your city's arena. Concert attendance is down, so you want to propose an act that will have people lining up for tickets. After scanning music and entertainment magazines and finding out the most popular song downloads, you draft a proposal for your boss, the arena's director of entertainment. Use hard facts to convince your boss to book the singer or band you suggest. Be sure to pay close attention to finding a clear, interesting topic for your proposal.

Role: special-events manager
Audience: director of entertainment
Format: a proposal
Topic: a musical act for your city's arena
Strong Verbs: draft, convince

Write your proposal on a separate sheet of paper. Before you begin to write, jot down some details you might include.

Chris Brown	He doesn't cost much
Chicago Stadium	Send money to homeless
Good singer	
Good Rapper Rapper	
Get some money	

Think About

- Have I chosen a topic that I really like?
- Do I have something new to say about this topic?
- Am I writing about what I know and care about?
- Have I gathered enough information about it so that I'm ready to write?

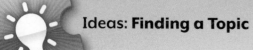

Jump Start Sheet

Unit Project Topic: _____

Days 1 and 3: My Unit Project To-Do List

- Wear protective gear for pearl
✓ • Feeding the poor
- Help less fortunate teens
- donate money to charity

Day 5: My Six-Word Statement on Responsibility

_____ _____ _____ _____ _____

Focus on Grammar and Usage

Find two sentences in your writing that contain the passive voice. Rewrite them in the active voice.

1. _____

   _____

   _____

2. _____

   _____

   _____

Write-On Sheet

R: Founder and president at EYC
A: Teens in my community
F: Persuasive Essay
T: Feeding the poor

-Intro (Lead-hook)
   Hook-

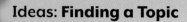

Preview

A Humor Writer

In the spaces below, fill in your thoughts about the job of a humor writer.

1. Think about the funniest thing you have ever seen or heard. What made it so funny?

   _____

   _____

   _____

   _____

2. Humor can come from unusual situations, uncomfortable scenarios, inside jokes, unexpected outbursts, and more. What's your favorite kind?

   _____

   _____

   _____

   _____

3. Humor writers have to be good with words and people and know lots about different subjects. What do you think the hardest part of the job is?

   _____

   _____

   _____

   _____

Bonus: Look up on the Internet what a humor writer does. Write your findings on note cards and share them with a classmate.

Warning: Cell Phone Overload

What happens when you talk or text too much on a cell phone?
Write four hazards in the boxes.

Now use your ideas to create three labels warning
teens about the dangers of cell phone addiction.

If u txt 2
mch yr rtng
is :-0 zzz

- **Creating the Lead**
- Using Sequence Words and Transition Words
- Structuring the Body
- Ending With a Sense of Resolution

Focus Mode: Persuasive
Theme: Responsibility

Organization

Organization is about how your idea unfolds from beginning to end—how you structure and arrange your details. An organized piece of writing begins engagingly, moves along logically, and ends satisfyingly. You give readers the right amount of information at the right moments. When your organization is working, following the idea is effortless.

Creating the Lead

You get one chance to make a good first impression with a piece of writing—and that is with your lead. Whether it's a fact, question, or quotation, a good lead introduces your topic to readers and assures them that you have a plan and a direction. It entices readers by providing a lively, tantalizing glimpse of what is to come.

I'm rooting for Team Organization. Go, O, Go!

Organization

How is the front-runner in a race like the lead in a piece of writing?

How to Write a Lead

The lead is your big chance to connect with your reader. So don't blow it! Here are some ideas for creating great ones.

1. Work Backward From Your Draft

Sometimes it's easier to write the lead *after* you've drafted the body of your piece. Elements of your piece that can inspire a great lead include:

- **direction**—where the piece is going to end up or conclude
- **content**—the different points the piece makes or elements it contains
- **tone**—a serious, sarcastic, confident, secure tone will influence the lead

2. Interview Yourself

No one knows more about your piece than you do. So ask yourself:

- Who is my reader?
- What will interest him or her most about my piece? How will he or she connect to it?

3. Put Yourself in the Role of Reader

If you were reading this piece, what would convince you? Ask yourself:

- What about this subject matters to you?
- What would make me want to pick it up and read it?

4. Choose a Technique

Once you've established the purpose, audience, and tone, choose an appropriate technique for writing the lead. Here are four to consider:

- **anecdote**—a brief, real-life scenario or story
- **analogy**—two or more different things compared
- **fact or statistic**—an interesting piece of information about your topic
- **summary**—a brief overview of what will be addressed

In the space below, write other techniques you have used successfully.

_____

_____

_____

R.A.F.T.S. 2

You are a student in a small town who is frustrated that there isn't a safe, inviting place in the community for teens like you to gather after school. Write an e-mail to the city council, proposing to repurpose an unused or little-used town space—such as a room of the library—especially for young people. Be sure to create a lead that will grab your audience's attention (and support!).

Role: student
Audience: city council members
Format: e-mail proposal
Topic: after-school space for teens
Strong Verbs: propose, secure

Write your proposal on a separate sheet of paper. Before you begin, jot down some details you might include.

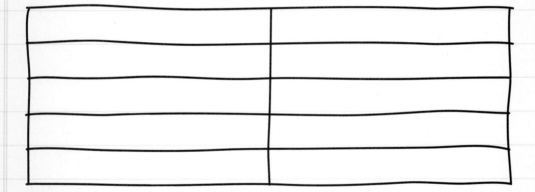

Think About

- Did I give the reader something interesting to think about right from the start?
- Will the reader want to keep reading?
- Have I tried to get the reader's attention?
- Did I let the reader know what is coming?

Organization: Creating the Lead

Jump Start Sheet

Days 1 and 3: My Unit Project To-Do List

- _____
- _____
- _____
- _____

Day 5: My Six-Word Statement on Responsibility

_____ _____ _____ _____ _____ _____

Focus on Word Study

Root: *tele*

Meaning: _____

Common Words That Contain the Root:

1.

2.

3.

My Wacky Word

_____

_____

_____

_____

_____

Write-On Sheet

The date is 5/26/13. Hundreds and thousands of people coming together to feed the poor in elk grove villaage. Imagin the smiles on peoples faces as they get something that they been longing for. FOOD! EYC is going to conduct a program about feeding the poor. You can see this amazing site if you can let us areana.

Background

Thesis

Teen ~~peole~~ should take action to volentior to help EYC to feeed the poor. (Thesis)

Preview

Joan Bauer, author of *Peeled*

In the spaces below, answer the questions about Joan Bauer.

1. Joan Bauer said that as a child, she had a fascination with humor—and she still does. How do you think that fascination might influence her work, even when she's writing about a serious topic?

   _____

   _____

2. Joan Bauer has said that she often felt awkward and different growing up. How might that experience help a writer create interesting characters?

   _____

   _____

   _____

3. Joan Bauer's grandmother had a particularly strong influence on her writing. Who influences your writing? How so?

   _____

   _____

   _____

4. A common theme in Joan Bauer's books is overcoming adversity. Is this a theme to which you can relate? Why or why not?

   _____

   _____

   _____

In Response

A good lead is so "a-peeling"!

Now that you've heard a bit of *Peeled*, imagine you were in the audience when Martin delivered his speech. Draft the body of your response. Then work backward from it to write a lead.

Draft of the Body

_____

_____

_____

_____

_____

My Lead

_____

_____

_____

_____

_____

The Lead Technique I Used and Why I Think It Is Effective

_____

_____

_____

_____

- **Establishing a Tone**
- Conveying the Purpose
- Creating a Connection to the Audience
- Taking Risks to Create Voice

Focus Mode: Persuasive
Theme: Responsibility

Voice

Voice is the energy and attitude of a piece of writing. In fiction, voice can take on almost any tone, from humorous or hopeful to serious or somber. In nonfiction, it is often compelling, authoritative, and knowledgeable. You arrive at the right voice for a piece by thinking deeply about your purpose and audience for it. You "speak" in a way that connects to your audience.

Establishing a Tone

My favorite station is WTMN, Trait Mate News, 24/7.

Voice

When you speak, you express how you feel with the tone of your voice. The same is true for writing. When you establish a tone that is compelling and right for the piece, readers feel your conviction. They want to keep reading because they feel you're speaking directly to them. Multiple tones can be present in a single piece; it's the sum of the tones that creates voice.

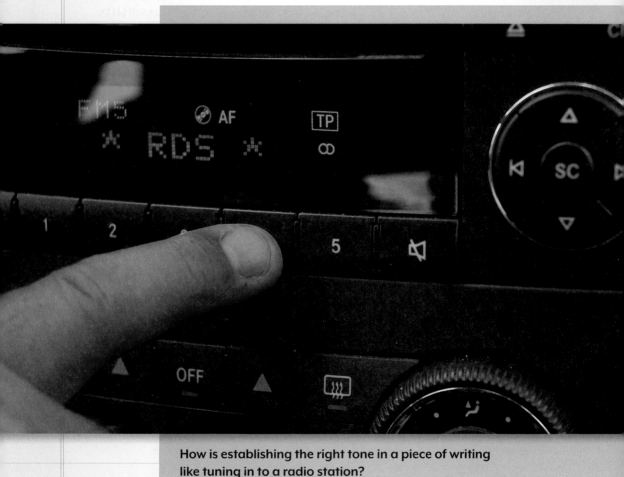

How is establishing the right tone in a piece of writing like tuning in to a radio station?

Tone Up Your Writing

To establish the tone of a piece of writing, imagine talking about your topic to a particular audience. Who are you talking to? How do you sound? Use the answers to hit just the right note.

Here are a variety of tones:

angry, anxious, calm, casual, concerned, curious, determined, excited, friendly, frightened, frustrated, passionate, proud, weary

Which of the listed tones would you use in each of the following situations?

1. Telling your best friend that your family is moving.

_____

2. Disagreeing with a grade your teacher gave you for an assignment.

_____

3. Convincing a parent to let you sign up for (or quit) an after-school activity.

_____

4. Letting your parents know that it's unfair of them to ask you to babysit your younger brother so often.

_____

Now pick one of the situations or one of your own and write a sentence or two that captures the tone(s) you chose.

_____

_____

_____

_____

_____

R.A.F.T.S. 3

You are the captain of your baseball team. Lately many of the players on the team have been skipping practices or coming late. You have a game in two weeks against the toughest team in the league, and if your team has any chance of winning, you need all hands on deck. Develop a strongly worded e-mail to send to your teammates to convince them to make practice a priority. Be sure to pay close attention to establishing a strong, convincing tone.

Role: captain of a baseball team
Audience: teammates on baseball team
Format: e-mail
Topic: importance of coming to practice
Strong Verbs: develop, send, convince

Write your e-mail on a separate sheet of paper. Before you begin to write, jot down some details you might include.

Think About

- Can I name the primary tone of my writing (for example, happy, frustrated, knowledgeable, scared, convincing)?
- Have I varied the tone from the beginning to the end, as necessary to convey my thoughts?
- Have I been expressive?
- Did I show that I care about this topic?

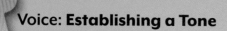

Jump Start Sheet

Unit Project Topic: _____

Days 1 and 3: My Unit Project To-Do List

- _____

- _____

- _____

- _____

Day 5: My Six-Word Statement on Responsibility

_____ _____ _____ _____ _____ _____

Focus on Grammar and Usage

Search your writing for sentences in which you have used dependent clauses and independent clauses incorrectly. Rewrite two of them correctly here. If you can't find any problems, write two new, correct sentences using dependent and independent clauses.

1. _____

_____

_____

2. _____

_____

_____

Write-On Sheet

Preview

John A. Stokes, author of *Students on Strike*

Answer the questions below, on your own or with a partner.

1. In 1951, John A. Stokes helped lead a strike at his high school to protest unequal educational opportunities for African-American students. Why do you think he chose to record his experiences in a memoir?

_____

_____

_____

_____

2. John A. Stokes is an educator and writer. His parents believed that having a good education was powerful. How do you think his upbringing and values are reflected in the adult choices he made?

_____

_____

_____

3. In the excerpt you are about to read, John A. Stokes talks about the influence his parents had on him and on his view of education. Write the name of a family member who has influenced you and a statement explaining how he or she influenced you.

_____

_____

_____

Bonus: Find more information about John A. Stokes on the Internet, or look up reviews of *Students on Strike*. Share what you learn with a classmate.

Name That Tone

An author's purpose for writing, intended audience, and feelings about the topic all help determine the tone of a piece. Fill in the tone of John A. Stokes's *Students on Strike* and a sentence that captures that tone. Then fill in his purpose, audience, and feelings about the topic. Did he establish the right tone, in your opinion?

Ever heard "Don't take that tone with me . . ."? Yeah, me too. Parents!

Voi

Tone:

_____

A Sentence From the Excerpt That Captures the Tone:

_____

Author's Audience:	**Author's Purpose:**	**Author's Feelings About the Topic:**
_____	_____	_____
_____	_____	_____

Now think about the family member you named on the Preview sheet who influenced you. On a separate sheet of paper, write a paragraph describing his or her influence and the ongoing effect it has had on you. Be sure to use an appropriate tone.

Persuasive Publishing Checklist

Think you are ready to go public with your extended persuasive project? Use this form to make sure you've covered all the writing bases.

I remembered to...

- [ ] state my position on the topic clearly and stick with it.

- [ ] offer good, sound reasoning that the reader can relate to easily.

- [ ] back up my argument with solid facts, details, and examples that are based on reliable, objective sources.

- [ ] expose weaknesses in other positions.

- [ ] develop my argument using solid reasoning from beginning to end.

- [ ] use a compelling, confident voice to add credibility.

- [ ] explain any unusual words, phrases, or concepts.

- [ ] read my piece aloud to check how it will sound to the reader.

- [ ] proofread my piece carefully and clean up problems with conventions.

I'm persuaded. You're great at traits, mate!

Conventions

The purpose of my piece is

_____

The most critical point I make is

_____

What I hope readers will take away from my piece is

_____

_____

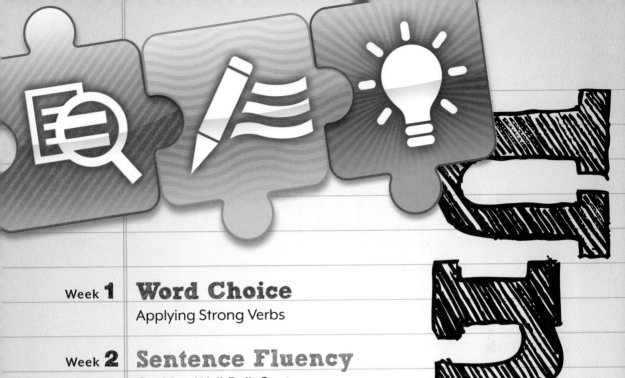

Focus Mode: Expository

The world is rich with interesting ideas to explore in writing. When you write in the expository mode, you give information about or explain a topic that fascinates you. Think about including captivating details, intriguing insights, and significant life experiences. The best expository writing has a strong, confident voice—a voice that tells the reader you know what you're talking about.

Unit 3

- **Applying Strong Verbs** ·····················
- Selecting Striking Words and Phrases
- Using Specific and Accurate Words
- Choosing Words That Deepen Meaning

Focus Mode: Expository
Theme: Mysteriousness

Word Choice

Words are the building blocks of writing. Well-chosen words bring your ideas into focus. They create images, spark the imagination, and grab the reader's attention. Word choice is verbal alchemy; it's how writers transform the ordinary into the extraordinary. Choose words that move, enlighten, and inspire.

I've been lifting verbs for years. These biceps don't lie.

Word Choice

Applying Strong Verbs

You can "eat"—or you can "nibble," "gobble," or "wolf down." Strong verbs deliver the power and punch that writing needs to be powerful. They capture action precisely in just one little word. When you use strong verbs, your writing is electrifying. It bursts with energy!

How are strong verbs in your writing like the well-developed muscles in a body?

Word Choice: Applying Strong Verbs

Verb Power

These techniques will help you choose strong verbs. Read each technique and its sample sentence. Circle the verb in the sample sentence and then write three other verbs to replace it: a strong one, a stronger one, and then the strongest one you can think of.

1. Use precise verbs to add punch and vigor.

Think about the action you are describing. Then choose verbs that capture that action perfectly.

We made birdhouses last week.

_____

_____

2. Use the active voice instead of the passive voice.

The passive voice contains forms of the verb *to be* (*am, is, are, was, were, be, being, been*), which can make your writing sound less dynamic.

The car was fixed by the mechanic.

_____

_____

3. Stretch to find unusual, out-of-the-ordinary verbs.

Don't settle for a ho-hum verb when there may be one out there that helps your reader visualize the action.

Sara put the vase on the table.

_____

_____

4. Avoid adverbs. Instead, look for better, more descriptive verbs.

One vivacious verb packs more power than an array of adverbs.

The star tennis player completely beat her opponents.

_____

_____

R.A.F.T.S. 4

You are a country songwriter who's penned a number of smash hits. You've agreed to write a new song for the executives at Two Boots Records to produce, and the deadline is fast approaching. You've decided that your song will be about the mysteries of finding inspiration for your art. Reflect on that topic and relate what your heart tells you. Remember that active verbs give every line punch, so include as many as you can.

Role: country songwriter
Audience: record company executives
Format: first stanza of a song
Topic: mysteries of finding inspiration
Strong Verbs: reflect, record

Write the draft of your song on a separate sheet of paper. Before you begin to write, jot down some details you might include:

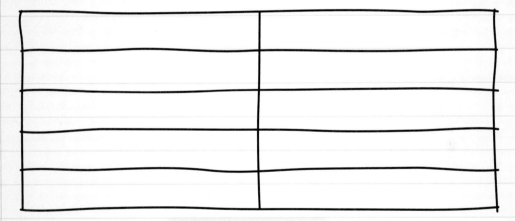

Think About

- Have I used action words?

- Did I stretch to get a better word—*scurry* rather than *run*?

- Do my verbs give my writing punch and pizzazz?

- Did I avoid *is, am, are, was, were, be, being,* and *been* whenever I could?

Jump Start Sheet

Unit Project Topic: _____

Days 1 and 3: My Unit Project To-Do List

- _____
- _____
- _____
- _____

Day 5: My Six-Word Statement on Mysteriousness

_____ _____ _____ _____ _____ _____

Focus on Word Study

Root: *therm*

Meaning: _____

Common Words That Contain the Root:

1.
2.
3.

My Wacky Word

_____

_____

_____

_____

Write-On Sheet

Word Choice: **Applying Strong Verbs**

A Cartoonist

Answer the questions below, on your own or with a partner.

1. The *Grand Avenue* comic strip you'll read on Day 4 is created by two prize-winning cartoonists. What do you think it takes to become a prize-winning cartoonist? What skills does it require?

   _____

   _____

   _____

2. Comics appear in books and newspapers, on the Internet, and even on bubble gum wrappers. Can you name other places you've seen comics?

   _____

   _____

   _____

3. What cartoon or comic strip do you particularly like? What appeals to you about it?

   _____

   _____

   _____

   _____

Bonus: Look on the Internet or in a newspaper for an editorial cartoon. What message does it give about current events? Write what you find out on note cards—or draw a cartoon!—and share them with a classmate.

Cartoon Craze

I have a few choice words about the cafeteria . . .

1. What funny message about cafeteria life could you relate in a cartoon? Write three ideas here. Circle the idea you like best.

_____

_____

_____

2. How do you picture your cartoon? In a single frame? In two frames like *Grand Avenue*? In three or four frames? Draw the frame(s) on a separate sheet of paper.

_____

_____

3. What characters will be in your cartoon?

_____

4. Brainstorm at least five strong verbs you might use in your cartoon.

_____

_____

_____

5. Sketch the illustrations and draft the text in the frame(s) you drew. Then revise and polish your cartoon on a clean sheet of paper.

- **Crafting Well-Built Sentences**
- Varying Sentence Types
- Capturing Smooth and Rhythmic Flow
- Breaking the "Rules" to Create Fluency

Focus Mode: Expository
Theme: Mysteriousness

Sentence Fluency

Writing may seem like a silent act, but it isn't. When you read your drafts, listen for passages that sound smooth and rhythmic . . . and passages that don't. From there, revise. By doing that, you'll create sentence fluency—the music of language that makes your writing sound as good as it looks.

Crafting Well-Built Sentences

With these wheels, there's no stopping me!

You should craft your sentences the way an automobile maker assembles an engine. That means writing sentences that are not all short or all long—and that start with different words, not the same word over and over again. Well-built sentences move the reader through the piece.

How are well-built sentences like the parts of a high-performance race-car engine?

Sentence Impact

Well-built sentences are both grammatically correct and creative. Here are techniques you can use to craft them.

1. Synonymous Words or Phrases

Vary the wording when referring to the same person, object, or place within a paragraph.

Example: Have you tried dune sledding? The spine-tingling ride is one activity you simply must experience. Even if you don't like snow sledding, sliding on sand will thrill you.

2. Sentence Lengths

Use a combination of short, medium, and long sentences.

Example: White Sands National Monument, in New Mexico, has incredibly high dunes. Sledding is free! You can spend an entire day coasting down the sparkling white sand under the warm sun.

3. Alliteration and Parallelism

Construct series of words and/or phrases in a similar way and use alliteration. Begin lists with the same part of speech.

Example: You can use a store-bought snow saucer, waxed for maximum speed. Streamlined, flat-bottomed sleds also work. Or cardboard. Remember to:

- add the wax sealer
- check the steering mechanism
- test the brakes (if there are any!)

4. Conjunctions

Use conjunctions to combine short sentences into longer ones. Some conjunctions to consider: *after, although, and, but, either/or, even if, for, neither/nor, nor, not only/but also, or, since, so, yet,* and so on.

Example: Some of the dunes are pretty high, so be ready to huff and puff your way to the top. After you do that, sit or lie on your saucer, even if it makes you nervous. Point your feet downhill and never, ever go headfirst!

R.A.F.T.S. 5

You are an astronomer who has just discovered something astounding—a previously unidentified moon orbiting Jupiter. Write an announcement proclaiming your discovery for next month's edition of *Astronomers Magazine*. Be sure to include specific details from your notes, to lend authenticity and to explain the mystery of why that moon was never spotted before. Remember to craft your sentences carefully.

Role: astronomer
Audience: scientific community
Format: announcement
Topic: discovery of a moon orbiting Jupiter
Strong Verb: proclaim

Write your announcement on a separate sheet of paper. Before you begin to write, jot down some details you might include.

Think About

- Do my sentences begin in different ways?
- Are my sentences of different lengths?
- Are my sentences grammatically correct, unless constructed creatively for impact?
- Have I used conjunctions to connect parts of sentences?

Jump Start Sheet

Days 1 and 3: My Unit Project To-Do List

- _____

- _____

- _____

- _____

Day 5: My Six-Word Statement on Mysteriousness

_____ _____ _____ _____ _____ _____

Focus on Grammar and Usage

Look through your work for sentences in which you've used singular and compound subjects and predicates incorrectly. Revise two of those sentences here.

1. _____

   _____

   _____

   _____

2. _____

   _____

   _____

   _____

Write-On Sheet

Preview

Mark Teague, author of *The Doom Machine*

Answer the questions below, on your own or with a partner.

1. What images does the title *The Doom Machine* conjure up for you? What do you think might happen in this story?

_____

_____

_____

2. With this story, Mark Teague proves he is a master of the mysterious. What other mysterious stories have you read? What moves did the writer make to create a sense of mystery?

_____

_____

_____

3. Mark Teague has also written *LaRue Across America: Postcards From the Vacation; The Secret Shortcut; How I Spent My Summer Vacation;* and *Moog Moog, Space Barber.* Based on their titles, which book would you most like to read? Why? If you have already read one of these books, or another book by Mark Teague, name it and explain how you feel about it.

_____

_____

_____

Bonus: Search on the Internet for information about Mark Teague. On note cards, write three interesting things you learned about him and share them with a classmate.

What Makes
The Doom Machine Hum?

Just doom it!

With a partner, complete the grid by thinking about each technique and finding at least one example from *The Doom Machine* excerpt that demonstrates how Teague applied it. Then answer the questions.

Sentence Fluency

Technique for Crafting Well-Built Sentences	Example
1. Use synonymous words and phrases.	
2. Vary the lengths and types of sentences.	
3. Use alliteration and parallelism.	
4. Connect sentence parts with conjunctions.	

Summarize Teague's sentence-crafting style. Think as a book reviewer would, by addressing not only which techniques he uses, but *how* he uses them.

_____

_____

What does all this mean for your writing? How can you apply to your own sentence fluency what you've learned about Teague's handling of that trait?

_____

_____

- Finding a Topic
- **Focusing the Topic** ··
- Developing the Topic
- Using Details

Focus Mode: Expository
Theme: Mysteriousness

Ideas

Ideas are your central message—the main thoughts you want to share. To make your ideas strong, choose a topic you care about and focus on one interesting aspect of it. From there, weave in original and unexpected details to open your readers' eyes and show them something they might otherwise overlook.

Focusing the Topic

Focusing a topic is like merging onto a freeway. There are many ideas to choose from, just as there are many lanes to choose from. But sticking to one lane allows you to go where you want to go in the same way focusing your topic allows you to take readers where you want them to go. You can relax, knowing they won't get lost.

What do the finalists in a play-off have in common with a focused topic in a piece of writing?

Would You Live HERE?

Answer these questions about an unusual or mysterious place you've visited or heard about.

1. What is the name of the place—or what do *you* call it?

_____

_____

2. How did you learn about it?

_____

_____

3. What makes it unusual or mysterious? Why are you fascinated by it?

_____

_____

4. How do you feel when you visit it or think about it?

_____

_____

5. What interesting things have happened there?

_____

_____

6. What questions do you have about it? What do you wonder about it?

_____

_____

R.A.F.T.S. 6

You are a mischievous and playful ferret. Your human owners have been leaving things like keys, socks, and cell phones around the house. You can't resist temptation, so you take them and stash them away in nooks and crannies in almost every room. In a series of anonymous notes to your owners, reveal clues to the locations of their belongings. Guide them to take back what's theirs—as much as you'd like to keep it!

Role: ferret
Audience: human owners
Format: notes
Topic: clues for finding missing items
Strong Verbs: reveal, guide

Write your notes on a separate sheet of paper. Before you begin to write, jot down some details you might include.

Think About

- Have I zeroed in on one small part of a bigger idea?
- Can I sum up my idea in a simple sentence?
- Have I chosen information that captures my idea best?
- Have I thought deeply about what the reader will need to know?

Jump Start Sheet

Days 1 and 3: My Unit Project To-Do List

- _____
- _____
- _____
- _____

Day 5: My Six-Word Statement on Mysteriousness

_____ _____ _____ _____ _____ _____

Focus on Word Study

Root: *arch*

Meaning: _____

Common Words That Contain the Root:

1.

2.

3.

My Wacky Word

_____

_____

_____

_____

_____

Write-On Sheet

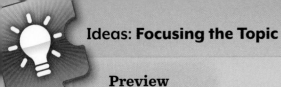

Ideas: **Focusing the Topic**

Preview

N. B. Grace, author of
UFOs: What Scientists Say May Shock You!

Answer the questions below, on your own or with a partner.

1. What kind of information about aliens might be shocking to some readers? What would be shocking to you? Why?

   _____

   _____

   _____

   _____

2. N. B. Grace wanted to be a writer since she was seven years old, but calls her path to publication "a long marathon" that includes lots of side trips. What does that tell you about her as a person and a writer?

   _____

   _____

   _____

   _____

3. N. B. Grace has also written *Camp Rock: Second Session #7, Mummies Unwrapped: The Science Behind Mummy Making*, and *Women in Space (Girls Rock!)*. Based on the titles, which book would you like to read? Why?

   _____

   _____

   _____

   _____

What Do You Think?

Answer these questions to identify N. B. Grace's focused topic for "Kidnapped: Could Thousands of People All Be Wrong?" and to determine if she provides enough evidence for you to believe that alien abductions are real.

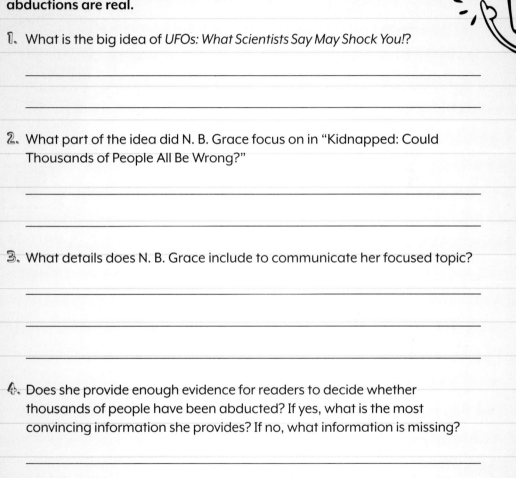

I was abducted by aliens once. They found me puzzling.

1. What is the big idea of *UFOs: What Scientists Say May Shock You!?*

   _____

   _____

2. What part of the idea did N. B. Grace focus on in "Kidnapped: Could Thousands of People All Be Wrong?"

   _____

   _____

3. What details does N. B. Grace include to communicate her focused topic?

   _____

   _____

4. Does she provide enough evidence for readers to decide whether thousands of people have been abducted? If yes, what is the most convincing information she provides? If no, what information is missing?

   _____

   _____

   _____

   _____

Expository Publishing Checklist

Think you are ready to go public with your expository unit project? Use this form to make sure you've covered all the writing bases.

I remembered to

☐ include intriguing and accurate facts that came from reliable sources.

☐ weave in details that go beyond the obvious and show how much I know about my topic.

☐ choose a text structure that supports my big idea and makes my message clear.

☐ anticipate and answer readers' questions and help them make personal connections.

☐ develop the topic logically from beginning to end.

☐ use a compelling voice that expresses my fascination for the topic.

☐ explain any unusual words, phrases, or concepts.

☐ read my piece aloud to check how it will sound to the reader.

☐ proofread my piece carefully and clean up problems with conventions.

The purpose of my piece is

_____

The part that works the best is

_____

What I hope readers will take away from my piece is

_____

From my perspective, your writin' is rockin'!

Presentation

Focus Mode: Narrative

Since the start of human history, people have been
telling stories to make sense of the world. When you
write in the narrative mode, you tell a story—either
a made-up one (fiction) or a real one (nonfiction).
Your stories should include characters, a setting, a
timeline, and a problem and its solution. Along the
way, they may include a surprise or two. And they
should always capture your reader's interest and
hang on to it, right to the end.

- Creating the Lead
- **Using Sequence Words and Transition Words** • • • • • • • • • • • • • • • • • • •
- Structuring the Body
- Ending With a Sense of Resolution

Focus Mode: Narrative
Theme: Success

Organization

Organization is about how your idea unfolds from beginning to end—how you structure and arrange your details. An organized piece of writing begins engagingly, moves along logically, and ends satisfyingly. You give readers the right amount of information at the right moments. When your organization is working, following the idea is effortless.

Using Sequence Words and Transition Words

That's a bike chain? Wheely?

Organization

Sequence words (such as *before* and *later*) and transition words (such as *however* and *because*) show how ideas progress, relate, and/or diverge. When you weave sequence and transition words into a piece, your sentences fit together seamlessly. It's easy to see relationships among your ideas.

How are sequence and transition words like the links in a bicycle chain?

Get Connected

Sequence words and transition words strengthen the connections between ideas in your writing—and, therefore, the overall organization of your piece. Here are a few you can use at the beginning, middle, or end of your sentences. Add others that you know.

To add an idea

also, again, besides, moreover, furthermore, in addition, similarly

Example: Elle is smart and funny in addition to being kind.

To show a result

accordingly, as a result, consequently, therefore, subsequently, thus

Example: Jonah waited until the last minute to write his report. He was up past midnight, consequently, writing it the night before it was due.

To provide examples

for example, for instance, in this case, for one thing

Example: Desmond is very considerate. For instance, he always holds the door for his teachers and classmates.

To show order

next, soon, then, at first, after, at last, meanwhile, finally, indeed, therefore, to sum up

Example: After you beat the butter and sugar, add two eggs.

To show direction

here, there, under, above, to the left, to the right, beyond, over there

Example: Beyond the last house on our street, there are thick woods.

R.A.F.T.S. 7

You are a journalist for a newspaper. Your city has a mysterious superhero who uses inexplicable powers to fight crime. Last night, this hero stopped a jewel thief who was trying to steal the world's largest diamond from the vault of the Indaruf Casino. You need to write an eye-catching article for the newspaper to report what happened, including when, where, and how the villain was stopped. Be sure to use sequence and transition words to clarify the order of events.

Role: journalist
Audience: newspaper readers
Format: an article
Topic: Indaruf Casino robbery intervention by local superhero
Strong Verbs: write, report

Write your article on a separate sheet of paper. Before you begin to write, jot down some details you might include.

Think About

- Have I used sequence words such as *later*, *then*, and *meanwhile*?

- Did I use a variety of transition words such as *however*, *because*, *also*, and *for instance*?

- Have I shown how the ideas connect from sentence to sentence?

- Does my organization make sense from paragraph to paragraph?

Jump Start Sheet

Unit Project Topic: _____

Days 1 and 3: My Unit Project To-Do List

- _____
- _____
- _____
- _____

Day 5: My Six-Word Statement on Success

_____ _____ _____ _____ _____ _____

Focus on Grammar and Usage

Search your writing for sentences in which you have used the incorrect verb form. Rewrite two of them correctly here. Or, if you can't find any problems, write two that show you really know what you are doing with correct verb forms.

1. _____

_____

_____

_____

2. _____

_____

_____

_____

Write-On Sheet

Preview

Steve Sheinkin, author of
Two Miserable Presidents

Answer the questions below, on your own or with a partner.

1. When you see the title of Steve Sheinkin's mentor text, *Two Miserable Presidents*, what do you think it will be about?

_____

_____

_____

_____

2. Sheinkin taught school before he began writing books for young people. How do you think that experience helps him write books kids will enjoy?

_____

_____

_____

_____

3. Well regarded for his storytelling skills and attention to detail, Steve Sheinkin carries out meticulous research to make his work interesting. What lesser-known facts would you like to know about the presidents?

_____

_____

_____

_____

The Great Escape

Plan an escape that Robert Smalls might have made, using this chart to show the order of events, and sequence and transition words to show the connections between events.

I've got a super idea for the sequel: The Great TRAIT Escape!

Organization

- Establishing a Tone
- **Conveying the Purpose** ·································
- Creating a Connection to the Audience
- Taking Risks to Create Voice

Focus Mode: Narrative
Theme: Success

Voice

Voice is the energy and attitude of a piece of writing. In fiction, voice can take on almost any tone, from humorous or hopeful to serious or somber. In nonfiction, it is often compelling, authoritative, and knowledgeable. You arrive at the right voice for a piece by thinking deeply about your purpose and audience for it. You "speak" in a way that connects to your audience.

Conveying the Purpose

Hey, I want a cap, too. Are eye holes extra?

The voice you use should match your purpose for writing. For example, if your purpose is to tell a story about being lost in the wilderness, your voice might be desperate and suspenseful. You may want to use an authoritative voice when writing an expository piece and a convincing one for a persuasive piece. Use voice to help readers understand why you want them to listen.

Voice

How is conveying your purpose in writing like coaching a baseball team?

Keep the Purpose Clear

Before you can write with voice, you need to determine your purpose. For each purpose below, add two possible tones of voice. Then choose one writing example and an appropriate tone. Write two sentences in that tone of voice that could be used to begin the piece and make the purpose clear.

1. To tell a story

Examples: a biography of someone you admire; a story about zombies that invade your school; a biographical snapshot about a time you broke a rule

Possible voices: heartfelt, creepy, hilarious _____

_____

_____

_____

2. To inform or explain

Examples: a magazine article about a totally green school; a blog post about a breakthrough in leukemia research; a science report for your chemistry experiment

Possible voices: knowledgeable, credible, expert _____

_____

_____

_____

3. To construct an argument

Examples: a letter to the highway department about posting walk signs near a school; a news article announcing the need for volunteers at a bird sanctuary; a poster for a city official's re-election

Possible voices: convincing, authoritative, compelling _____

_____

_____

_____

R.A.F.T.S. 8

A parent and teen are having a conversation. Last month, the parent was blown away by two low test grades the teen brought home, in pre-algebra and social studies. To avoid being grounded, the teen agreed to study extra hard and be more successful on the next tests. But it is now the weekend before the next tests, and he or she wants to go to the mall. Together with a partner—one as parent, one as teen—create a script of their conversation, in which each side reveals the reasons the teen should stay home or get to go. Remember to use the right voice to convey *your* character's purpose to its audience, the other character.

Role: parent (or child)
Audience: your child (or parent)
Format: conversation script
Topic: going to the mall vs. studying
Strong Verbs: create, reveal

Write your script on a separate sheet of paper. Before you begin to write, jot down some details you might include.

Think About

- Is the purpose of my writing clear?
- Does my point of view come through?
- Is this the right tone for this kind of writing?
- Have I used strong voice throughout this piece?

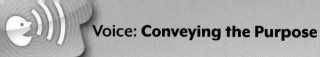

Jump Start Sheet

Unit Project Topic: _____

Days 1 and 3: My Unit Project To-Do List

- _____
- _____
- _____
- _____

Day 5: My Six-Word Statement on Success

_____ _____ _____ _____ _____ _____

Focus on Word Study

Root: *eco*
Meaning: _____

Common Words That Contain the Root:

1.
2.
3.

My Wacky Word

_____

_____

_____

_____

Write-On Sheet

Preview

An Entrepreneur

Answer the questions below, on your own or with a partner.

1. An entrepreneur creates products or offers services that will appeal to a particular audience. What makes this an interesting job?

_____

_____

_____

_____

2. Name a product that is appealing to you. What makes it appealing?

_____

_____

_____

_____

3. Name a product that you want to own. How did you hear about it? What makes it so appealing to you?

_____

_____

_____

_____

Bonus: Look up on the Internet what an entrepreneur does. Write your findings on note cards and share them with a classmate.

Sweet Success

Don't be modest, dude. Show them your brilliance for business.

Answer the questions below and use your answers to write the success story of the company that created your product.

1. What is the story of the origin of your company?

   _____

   _____

   _____

2. How did the company get its name?

   _____

   _____

   _____

3. What products made your company successful? What made them so popular?

   _____

   _____

   _____

4. What words best capture the spirit of your company or product?

   _____

   _____

   _____

- Applying Strong Verbs
- **Selecting Striking Words and Phrases** ••••••••••••••••••••••••••••••••
- Using Specific and Accurate Words
- Choosing Words That Deepen Meaning

Focus Mode: Narrative
Theme: Success

Word Choice

Words are the building blocks of writing. Well-chosen words bring your ideas into focus. They create images, spark the imagination, and grab the reader's attention. Word choice is verbal alchemy; it's how writers transform the ordinary into the extraordinary. Choose words that move, enlighten, and inspire.

Selecting Striking Words and Phrases

Speaking of striking, watch where you're pointing that umbrella!

Word Choice

When you use striking words and phrases, readers feel they're inside your idea, rather than sitting on the sidelines. Striking words and phrases, which include figurative language such as alliteration, simile, and metaphor, add dimension to your writing. Your piece lingers in readers' minds long after they've finished reading it.

How are striking words and phrases like multicolored umbrellas?

Go for Great

The words you choose take your writing to the next level—from ordinary to extraordinary. Here are some techniques for coming up with striking words and phrases. Read each example and write one of your own.

1. String words together.

Combine words in unusual ways to use as modifiers.

Example: After acing a math test and scoring the winning goal in the soccer game, my can't-get-any-better day did get better when Dad brought home Choco Cherry Yum ice cream.

Your Turn:

_____

2. Create new words.

Merge word parts or make up a word from scratch to make a point or add emphasis. Make them fun; keep them understandable.

Example: Those raw, foggy days that most people hate, I find *fantabulous.* Sure they cramp my outdoor plans, but they make my soul sing.

Your Turn:

_____

3. Use words in unusual ways.

Use common words in uncommon ways to create vivid descriptions.

Example: After her crowd-pleasing ballet recital, my little sister twinkled into the room, full of pride.

Your Turn:

_____

4. Use everyday words wisely.

Use simple words with clarity and specificity to create a natural voice.

Example: Her already pink cheeks deepened to red when the new boy entered the room.

Your Turn:

_____

R.A.F.T.S. 9

You are the inventor of levitating stationary running shoes, your greatest creation to date. R.A.D. (Real Action Dynamics), the world's biggest sporting goods company, wants to buy your invention, and you've made it through step 1: demonstrating to the executive committee of R.A.D. how the shoes work. In a monologue delivered to your assistant, tell the story of what happened when you demonstrated the shoes for the committee.

Role: inventor
Audience: assistant
Format: monologue
Topic: your presentation of an invention
Strong Verbs: delivered, tell

Write your monologue entry on a separate sheet of paper. Before you begin to write, jot down some details you might include.

Think About

- Did I try to use words that sound *just right*?
- Did I try hyphenating several shorter words to make an interesting-sounding new word?
- Did I try putting words with the same sound together?
- Did I read my piece aloud to find at least one or two moments I love?

Word Choice: Selecting Striking Words and Phrases

Jump Start Sheet

Unit Project Topic: _____

Days 1 and 3: My Unit Project To-Do List

- _____

- _____

- _____

- _____

Day 5: My Six-Word Statement on Success

_____ _____ _____ _____ _____ _____

Focus on Grammar and Usage

Search your writing for sentences in which you have used incorrect plural noun forms. Then revise two of those sentences here, using the correct plural noun form.

1. _____

   _____

   _____

   _____

2. _____

   _____

   _____

   _____

Write-On Sheet

Word Choice: **Selecting Striking Words and Phrases**

Preview
Tim Green, author of *Football Hero*

Answer the questions below on your own or with a partner.

1. Before Tim Green became a writer, he was a top defensive player for the NFL team the Atlanta Falcons. How do you think his experience as a football player helps him write realistically about athletes?

_____

_____

_____

_____

2. Tim Green enjoys visiting schools to talk about writing. If he were to visit your school, what would you ask him?

_____

_____

_____

_____

3. In addition to being an athlete and a writer, Tim Green has also been a radio and television commentator who wrote his own material. How might his career in broadcasting have helped him hone his writing voice?

_____

_____

_____

_____

Be a Winner

No "How a Winner Smells" column? Who's in charge here?!

Word Choice

Imagine that Thane from *Football Hero* is going to give a speech to Ty's team. The topic: what it means to be a winner. Use this planner to gather information to write the speech.

What a Winner Thinks	How a Winner Acts	What a Winner Does	How a Winner Feels

How is success related to being a winner?

_____

_____

_____

_____

_____

Narrative Publishing Checklist

Think you are ready to go public with your narrative unit project? Use this form to make sure you've covered all the writing bases.

I remembered to

Nifty narrative! And I'm not just saying that.

- [ ] present a clear, well-developed story line.
- [ ] include fascinating characters that grow and change over time.
- [ ] convey time and setting that make sense for the story.
- [ ] entertain, surprise, and challenge the reader.
- [ ] develop the story chronologically or take a risk to try a structure that also helps the reader follow the story easily.
- [ ] use an active voice to engage the reader.
- [ ] choose words that fit the characters, time, and place.
- [ ] read my piece aloud to check for places where I should speed up or slow down.
- [ ] proofread my piece carefully and clean up problems with conventions.

The purpose of my piece is

_____

My favorite part is

_____

What I hope readers will find most memorable about my piece is

_____

Focus Mode: Persuasive

If you want to be heard, it's important to know how to construct an argument. When you write in the persuasive mode, you write to convince the reader to agree with—or at least respect—your opinion on an important topic. You should clearly state your topic and position at the beginning and, from there, defend your position, using solid facts, irrefutable evidence, and a confident tone.

- Crafting Well-Built Sentences
- **Varying Sentence Types** . . . .
- Capturing Smooth and Rhythmic Flow
- Breaking the "Rules" to Create Fluency

Focus Mode: Persuasive
Theme: Hope

Sentence Fluency

Writing may seem like a silent act, but it isn't. When you read your drafts, listen for passages that sound smooth and rhythmic . . . and passages that don't. From there, revise. By doing that, you'll create sentence fluency— the music of language that makes your writing sound as good as it looks.

Varying Sentence Types

What if every piece of writing you pick up contains sentences that follow the same pattern: adjective, noun, verb, adverb? *Bor*-ing! A monotonous rhythm wracks your brain. Now imagine a piece with simple and compound sentences and with statements, questions, and exclamations. Mesmerizing! That's sentence variety.

Sentence Fluency

How is a variety of sentences like different types of pasta?

Simply Sublime Sentences

Writers use different types of sentences for different purposes. They may use long sentences for detailed explanations and short sentences to make a key point. As a result, they create a rhythm and flow that are pleasing to the reader's ear.

As you read the following examples, keep in mind that a sentence is made up of clauses.

An **independent clause** contains at least one subject and one verb. It can stand alone as a sentence.

A **dependent clause** cannot stand alone as a sentence because it doesn't contain a subject and a verb.

1. Simple Sentences

A simple sentence is made up of one independent clause. It may also contain a direct object or a prepositional phrase.

Examples: I buy CDs. I bought a CD on my birthday.

2. Compound Sentences

A compound sentence contains two or more independent clauses. Conjunctions such as *and, or, but, yet,* and *however* join the clauses.

Example: I buy CDs, but my brother downloads songs.

3. Complex Sentences

A complex sentence has one independent clause and one or more dependent clauses.

Example: When songs became available for purchase on the Internet, the music industry changed.

4. Compound-Complex Sentences

A compound-complex sentence has two or more independent clauses and at least one dependent clause.

Example: When some musicians refused to allow their songs to be sold on the Internet, their fans became upset, and those musicians began supporting the practice of downloading.

R.A.F.T.S. 10

You are a car hoping to be named No. 1 Teen Car of the Year. Write a contest entry paragraph about yourself—including your safety features—to ease the concerns of anxious parents. Convince teenagers that *you* are the car that will make them very happy drivers. Remember that having a variety of sentence types makes a paragraph easier to read, and the subject all the more tantalizing.

Role: car
Audience: teenage drivers
Format: contest entry
Topic: why you should be No. 1 Teen Car of the Year
Strong Verb: convince

Write your contest entry on a separate sheet of paper. Before you begin to write, jot down some details you might include.

Think About

- Did I include different kinds of sentences?
- Are some of my sentences complex?
- Are some of my sentences simple?
- Did I intermingle sentence types, one to the next?

Jump Start Sheet

Unit Project Topic: _____

Days 1 and 3: My Unit Project To-Do List

- _____

- _____

- _____

- _____

Day 5: My Six-Word Statement on Hope

_____ _____ _____ _____ _____ _____

Focus on Word Study

Root: *urb*
Meaning: _____
Common Words That Contain the Root:

1.

2.

3.

My Wacky Word

_____

_____

_____

_____

Write-On Sheet

Preview

Video Author

Answer the questions below, on your own or with a partner.

1. Many different types of videos use text as part of the presentation (documentaries, interviews, commentaries, spoken-word performances, and so on). What types have you seen and what are your favorites?

   _____

   _____

   _____

   _____

2. Have you ever created a video that required a transcript? How do you think writing for a video might differ from other writing you've done?

   _____

   _____

   _____

   _____

3. What traits do you think would matter most when writing for a video that will be read aloud?

   _____

   _____

   _____

   _____

Bonus: Look on the Internet for information about video scripts or video creation. Write notes about a video that interests you and share your notes with a classmate.

Reverse Writing

Capitalize and punctuate both versions of the poem below so they read fluently and convey different meanings. Then, think of one title that fits both of them.

!writing reverse like I

Forward:

why
when you hear bad news
you can find a road out
whenever
you want to go
great

Reverse:

great
you want to go
whenever
you can find a road out
when you hear bad news
why

My title for both versions:

_____

_____

How do capitalization, punctuation, and phrasing affect meaning? What might this mean for your own writing?

_____

_____

_____

_____

_____

_____

_____

_____

- Finding a Topic
- Focusing the Topic
- **Developing the Topic** ·····················
- Using Details

Focus Mode: Persuasive
Theme: Hope

Ideas

Ideas are your central message—the main thoughts you want to share. To make your ideas strong, choose a topic you care about and focus on one interesting aspect of it. From there, weave in original and unexpected details to open your readers' eyes and show them something they might otherwise overlook.

I just hope some dog doesn't come by and, you know, ruin it.

Developing the Topic

When you develop your topic, you expand your main idea in a logical direction. You give your story an original, unpredictable plot. You present accurate facts and relevant details in your nonfiction pieces. Your readers believe what you have to say because you say it in a way that is unique, credible, and enlightening.

Ideas

How is creating sidewalk art like developing the topic in a piece of writing?

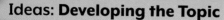

Topic Workout

Here are some techniques for developing a topic. Think about how they are applied below in the examples for the topic: "The Gettysburg Address: Lincoln's Great American Speech." Then, try them out on your own topic.

1. Support your topic with critical evidence.

Use reliable sources such as university or government websites, interviews with experts, and scholarly texts. Delve into diaries, letters, and reports.

Example: According to the Library of Congress website, President Lincoln gave the Gettysburg Address on November 19, 1863, as part of the dedication of the Soldiers' National Cemetery in Gettysburg, Pennsylvania.

2. Bring your own insights to the topic.

Let your readers know what interests you about the topic. If a small detail makes you curious, play it up. Don't be afraid to highlight what fascinates you.

Example: Lincoln had no advance warning that the first speaker, Edward Everett, would drone on for two hours. Lincoln's two-minute speech captured the listeners' attention in a way that Everett's did not.

3. Share memories and experiences.

Enhance your piece with memories and experiences related to your topic.

Example: Viewing Lincoln's words in his own handwriting made the Gettysburg Address come alive for me. It was as powerful as the time I visited the battleground itself and saw the graveyard there.

4. Ask yourself, "What questions might a reader have?" Answer those questions in your writing.

Ask these trusty, basic questions: *who? what? when? where? why? how?*

Example: How was Lincoln's speech received? Many people listened to and agreed with his message.

5. Weed out details that don't support your topic.

Interesting? Sure. Necessary? Nope. Pare down to the essentials.

Example: Everett was given forty days to write his speech; Lincoln was invited to speak at the ceremony just seventeen days in advance.

R.A.F.T.S. 11

You are a site where a historical event took place. However, your part in this event is not widely known, so you don't get many visitors or much attention. You hope to get more. Write an article, to be published by your local newspaper both in print and online, requesting more publicity. Explain why you should get more recognition and suggest ways to get it. Remember, a well-developed topic will draw readers in.

Role: historical site
Audience: community members
Format: newspaper article
Topic: historical importance and reasons for deserving more publicity
Strong Verbs: request, explain, suggest

Write your article on a separate sheet of paper. Before you begin to write, jot down some details you might include.

Think About

- Am I sure my information is right?
- Are my details chock-full of interesting information?
- Have I used details that show new thinking about this topic?
- Will my reader believe what I say about this topic?

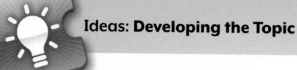

Ideas: Developing the Topic

Jump Start Sheet

Days 1 and 3: My Unit Project To-Do List

- _____
- _____
- _____
- _____

Day 5: My Six-Word Statement on Hope

_____ _____ _____ _____ _____ _____

Focus on Grammar and Usage

Search your writing for sentences in which you've used adverbs incorrectly.
Revise two of those sentences here.

1. _____

  _____

  _____

  _____

2. _____

  _____

  _____

  _____

Write-On Sheet

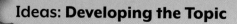

Ideas: **Developing the Topic**

Preview

James L. Swanson, author of
Chasing Lincoln's Killer

Answer the questions below, on your own or with a partner.

1. How does the title of the book help you identify the topic? What do you expect to learn from the book?

   _____

   _____

2. How might Swanson's educational background in history and law have helped him write this book?

   _____

   _____

3. On his tenth birthday, James L. Swanson received a copy of a newspaper article written the day after Lincoln was assassinated, which fueled his fascination with the event. What event in history would you like to know more about?

   _____

   _____

4. Using original sources, such as diaries and newspaper articles, to write historical fiction and nonfiction is important. Why?

   _____

   _____

Bonus: Look on the Internet to find more about James L. Swanson. Write your findings on note cards and share them with a classmate.

Tracking Swanson's Topic

Does James L. Swanson's topic have muscle? Find examples and details of personal knowledge, insight, critical evidence, and a question from *Chasing Lincoln's Killer*.

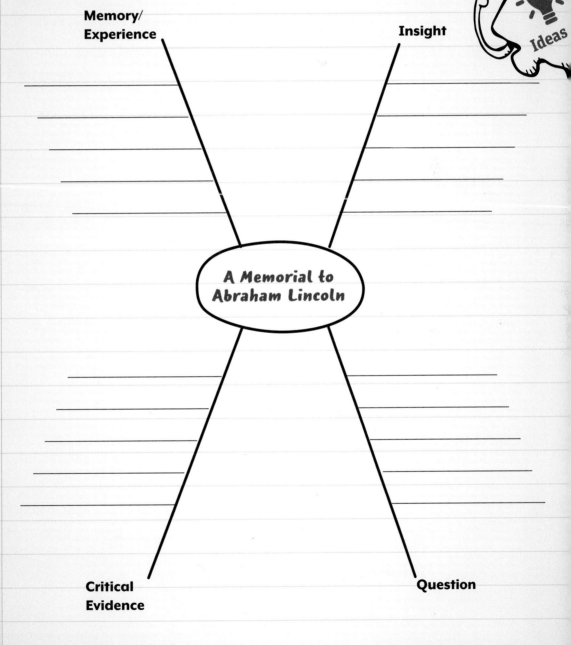

A tall hat and beard aren't for me. But Abe totally rocked that look. (Honestly, he did.)

Ideas

Memory/ Experience

Insight

A Memorial to Abraham Lincoln

Critical Evidence

Question

- Creating the Lead
- Using Sequence Words and Transition Words
- **Structuring the Body** ....
- Ending With a Sense of Resolution

Focus Mode: Persuasive
Theme: Hope

Organization

Organization is about how your idea unfolds from beginning to end— how you structure and arrange your details. An organized piece of writing begins engagingly, moves along logically, and ends satisfyingly. You give readers the right amount of information at the right moments. When your organization is working, following the idea is effortless.

Oh man, can you take over while I go on my lunch break?

Organization

Structuring the Body

When you structure the body of a piece of writing, you start with a foundation—the main idea. From there, you build the piece by fitting details together carefully and logically. You slow down your pace when you want readers to ponder a point and speed up when you want to move them along.

How is structuring the body of a piece of writing like building a hamburger?

Structuring for Success

When structuring the body of a piece of writing, consider these factors:

1. Order

To ensure that your piece reads smoothly and clearly, keep the overall text structure in mind as you introduce details and ideas. Arrange details in an order that makes sense—to show sequence, comparisons, cause and effect, order of importance, and so forth.

Examples: Manga and anime are two forms of "cartoon" art, hand-drawn or computer-generated. Manga is still-frames telling a story, for example, as in a graphic novel or comic book. Anime is moving pictures—the animated version of manga.

2. Logic

Tie details together so that readers understand their importance to the topic and how they relate to one another. Help readers build connections to the information you present as well as to things they may already know.

Examples: In the English-speaking world, manga and anime refer to examples of these art forms originating in Japan. In Japan, however, they refer to the art forms originating anywhere in the world. Comic books published in the United States, then, are manga; so are those published in China, Germany, or Australia.

3. Pacing

Lead readers through your piece at the appropriate velocity. Slow down to give them time to digest important points and details. Speed up to move readers along.

Examples: Although the popularity and sophistication of manga—and anime— are on the rise in the West, comic books in the United States have traditionally been aimed at a predominantly child-driven market: superheroes, cartoon animals, teenagers in comedic situations. Not so in Japan. There, manga has included serialized stories featuring realistic adults as fully developed characters. They have hopes and dreams . . . and flaws. They often make enormous mistakes that they need to absorb into their lives and carry on.

R.A.F.T.S. 12

You are a recently published novel for young adults. You have been placed on a list of books being considered for inclusion in the "YA Top 10" bookshelf in the school media center. Write a letter to the media specialist. Demonstrate why you should be selected as one of the books to be added to the shelves. Structure your letter carefully to make a perfect persuasive pitch.

Role: novel for young adults
Audience: school media specialist
Format: letter
Topic: placement on "YA Top 10" bookshelf in the media center
Strong Verbs: write, explain, selected

Write your letter on a separate sheet of paper. Before you begin to write, jot down some details you might include.

Think About

- Have I shown the reader where to slow down and speed up?
- Do all my details fit where I placed them?
- Will the reader find it easy to follow my ideas?
- Does the organization help my main idea stand out?

Jump Start Sheet

Days 1 and 3: My Unit Project To-Do List

- _____
- _____
- _____
- _____

Day 5: My Six-Word Statement on Hope

_____   _____   _____   _____   _____   _____

Focus on Word Study

Root: *anim*
Meaning: _____
Common Words That Contain the Root:

1.

2.

3.

My Wacky Word

_____

_____

_____

_____

_____

Write-On Sheet

Preview

David M. Schwartz, author of *G Is for Googol*

Answer the questions below, on your own or with a partner.

1. Math and science have been David M. Schwartz's primary interests since childhood. What do you think *G Is for Googol* is about? How do you think the text might be organized?

_____

_____

2. David M. Schwartz has said, "I cannot think of a better career than writing and speaking to children and their teachers." What do you think he finds so meaningful about that career?

_____

_____

3. *Where in the Wild?, Where Else in the Wild?, How Much Is a Million?,* and *If You Made a Million* are other books David M. Schwartz has written. Which of these would you be most interested in reading? Explain why.

_____

_____

4. If David M. Schwartz came to your school, what would you like him to talk about? What would you ask him?

_____

_____

Bonus: Look on the Internet to find out more about David M. Schwartz. Write on a note card something interesting you learn. Share it with a classmate.

S Is for Structure

Is "I Is for 'If'" structured well? Does David M. Schwartz use details, pacing, and logic expertly to organize the piece? Find out by answering the questions below.

O is for Organization. I'm just saying . . .

1. What is the main idea? How does the author order the details to support it?

_____

_____

_____

2. Are there any unnecessary details you could eliminate?

_____

_____

_____

3. Where does the author slow down to give you time to think?

_____

_____

_____

4. Where does he speed up to move you along?

_____

_____

_____

5. How does the author use logic to help you connect to what he's saying?

_____

_____

Persuasive Publishing Checklist

Think you are ready to go public with your persuasive unit project? Use this form to make sure you've covered all the writing bases.

Wait—you've got spinach between your teeth. Okay, NOW you're ready to go public!

I remembered to

☐ state my position on the topic clearly and stick with it.

☐ offer good, sound reasoning that the reader can relate to easily.

☐ back up my argument with solid facts, details, and examples that are based on reliable, objective sources.

☐ expose weaknesses in other positions.

☐ develop my argument using solid reasoning from beginning to end.

☐ use a compelling, confident voice to add credibility.

☐ explain any unusual words, phrases, or concepts.

☐ read my piece aloud to check how it will sound to the reader.

☐ proofread my piece carefully and clean up problems with conventions.

The purpose of my piece is

_____

The most critical point I make is

_____

What I hope readers will take away from my piece is

_____

_____

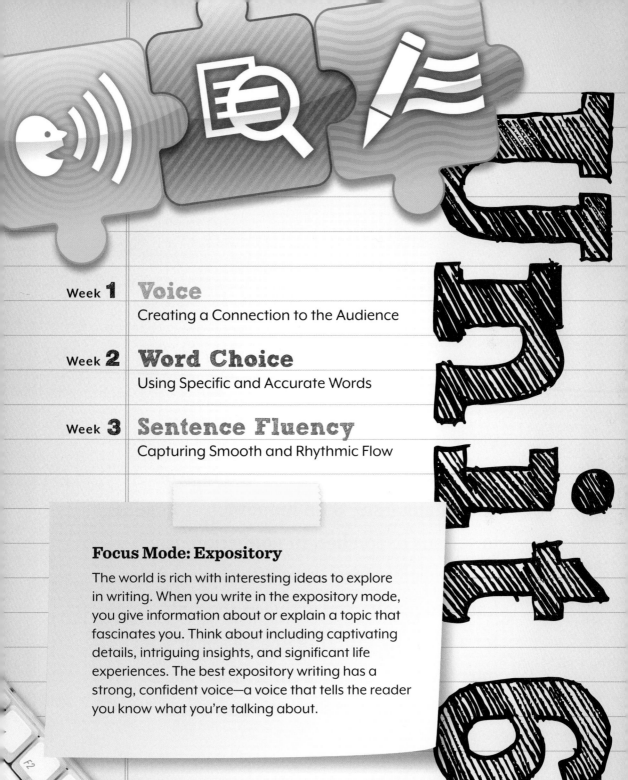

Focus Mode: Expository

The world is rich with interesting ideas to explore in writing. When you write in the expository mode, you give information about or explain a topic that fascinates you. Think about including captivating details, intriguing insights, and significant life experiences. The best expository writing has a strong, confident voice—a voice that tells the reader you know what you're talking about.

- Establishing a Tone
- Conveying the Purpose
- **Creating a Connection to the Audience** •••••••••••••••••••••••••••••••••
- Taking Risks to Create Voice

Focus Mode: Expository
Theme: Strength

Voice

Voice is the energy and attitude of a piece of writing. In fiction, voice can take on almost any tone, from humorous or hopeful to serious or somber. In nonfiction, it is often compelling, authoritative, and knowledgeable. You arrive at the right voice for a piece by thinking deeply about your purpose and audience for it. You "speak" in a way that connects to your audience.

A giant fuzzy green guy? Really? And you think a talking puzzle piece is strange . . .

Voice

Creating a Connection to the Audience

When you're speaking to your friends, you probably use different language and a different tone than when you're speaking to your English teacher. The same principle applies to writing. By saying just the right things in just the right way, you connect to readers. You make them want to listen and take your message seriously.

How is connecting with the audience in writing like connecting to the public at a sporting event?

Get Connected

The Voice trait shows that the writer has thought about the audience. Voice helps make ideas and information accessible. After all, connecting with the reader helps keep the reader reading! Here are ideas to help you connect.

1. Appeal to your readers at a personal level.

Talk about what matters to you and make it also matter to the reader. Feel free to reveal your feelings, but understand that readers may feel differently.

Example: Since Mom died, I've taken on more responsibility than my dad would like. But he works, and I need to pitch in. It's hard—some days I'd rather be shooting baskets! But dinner needs fixing and it's worth it to see the grins on my little brothers' faces when I serve their favorite—mac and cheese.

2. Use words and phrases that your reader will understand.

Avoid slang or jargon that may be unfamiliar or that only a select few would understand. ("BFF" is okay for your peers, but what about for someone who isn't slang-savvy?) Which of these works better for the general reader?

Version 1: He went 43-3 and won six titles, including three majors.

Version 2: He lost only three out of 43 matches, and three of his six victories were major tournaments.

3. Give examples or anecdotes that your readers can relate to.

Writers tell stories to make a point and give the reader something to connect with in the writing. Say what you want and make it interesting at the same time.

Example: I picked up the cookie box—light as a feather. A glance revealed two broken snickerdoodles inside. "Who puts back a box with two measly cookies?" I thought. "T-O-N-Y!" I yelled to my brother. Oh, it was him all right.

4. Make your writing approachable—use a nonjudgmental tone.

You may have strong feelings about a topic, but it's important not to rant or ramble, or readers may tune you out. Which is better?

Version 1: I'm very possessive about my room and my stuff. When my older sister "helps out" by straightening up, I don't feel grateful. I feel as if she is scolding me for my mess. I resent her invasion of my turf, and I always let her know! She means well, but in this case I think she should respect my privacy.

Version 2: I don't like it when my sister cleans up my room. I mean, I don't mess with her mess. It's like she's saying she's better than me, and that's unfair.

R.A.F.T.S. 13

You are a pet—a snake, rabbit, cat, dog, or other animal—and you are unhappy with the care you've been getting from your teen owners. It's not that your owners are *bad*. It's just that they don't understand what kind of relationship a teen and his or her pet are supposed to have. In other words, they think you're there to amuse and adore them, while to you, clearly, it's the other way around. Write an owner's manual from your point of view, explaining exactly the approach you think your owners should take toward your care. Remember that in order to get them to listen, you're going to have to recognize the feelings they already have about you as a pet.

Role: a pet
Audience: your teenage owners
Format: an owner's manual
Topic: caring for you (the pet)
Strong Verbs: instruct, explain, recognize

Write your owner's manual on a separate sheet of paper. Before you begin to write, jot down some details you might include.

Think About

- Have I thought about the reader?

- Is this the right voice for the target audience?

- Have I shown what matters most to me in this piece?

- Will the reader know how I think and feel about the topic?

Jump Start Sheet

Unit Project Topic: _____

Days 1 and 3: My Unit Project To-Do List

- _____
- _____
- _____
- _____

Day 5: My Six-Word Statement on Strength

_____ _____ _____ _____ _____ _____

Focus on Grammar and Usage

Review your writing, find sentences in which you've used the incorrect adjective form, and revise two of those sentences here.

1. _____
   _____
   _____
   _____

2. _____
   _____
   _____
   _____

Write-On Sheet

Preview

Public Affairs Writer

Answer the questions below, on your own or with a partner.

1. Public affairs writers often write the slogans for national issues, such as getting vaccinated against diseases, and community issues, such as gathering support to open a branch library. What is a local, national, or global cause you care about? Try writing a slogan for it here.

_____

_____

_____

2. Public affairs writers often include in their writing visuals, such as charts, tables, or pictures. How do words and visuals work together to connect to the audience?

_____

_____

_____

_____

3. Why do you think connecting to an audience is a particularly important part of a public affairs writer's job?

_____

_____

_____

_____

Bonus: Look up on the Internet what a public affairs writer does. Write your findings on note cards and share them with a classmate.

"Stick With It" Planner

Use this chart to brainstorm some times you had to "stick with it"—and what you learned from the experience.

Accepting my extraordinary gift of gab. Sticking with that has been tough.

Time I Had to "Stick With It"	Why It Was Hard	What I Learned	How I Would Approach It Differently Another Time

Choose one time you had to "stick with it"; summarize the event here.

_____

Think about creating a bumper sticker with a slogan that conveys your experience. What would it say? Who is your target audience?

_____

Now write your slogan on a separate sheet of paper. Make sure it would fit the size of your bumper sticker. As you draft, focus on what your audience will relate to. Once you arrive at the final wording, experiment with color and letter styles to make your slogan pop. Then design the bumper sticker featuring your slogan and think about how it might also fit a banner, T-shirt, mug, refrigerator magnet, or baseball cap.

- Applying Strong Verbs
- Selecting Striking Words and Phrases
- **Using Specific and Accurate Words** ....
- Choosing Words That Deepen Meaning

Focus Mode: Expository
Theme: Strength

Word Choice

Words are the building blocks of writing. Well-chosen words bring your ideas into focus. They create images, spark the imagination, and grab the reader's attention. Word choice is verbal alchemy; it's how writers transform the ordinary into the extraordinary. Choose words that move, enlighten, and inspire.

Using Specific and Accurate Words

I once met a guy named Bill Board. His personality was totally flat.

Word Choice

Specific and accurate words give readers the information they need to understand your writing. For example, saying "The bridge was long" doesn't inform the reader the way this does: "The bridge spanned the river at its widest point and was high enough to allow tall-masted schooners to pass underneath." Using words like these puts bite into your piece!

How is using specific and accurate words in your writing like posting a public message?

Word Choice: Using Specific and Accurate Words

Getting Them Right

Words are the building blocks of your message, so you must choose them carefully. When your words are specific and accurate, your message is solid—and your readers get it.

Here are some things that sometimes get in the way of choosing specific and accurate words.

Misused Words—words that don't mean what you think they do

This often happens when you pick the longest, most impressive word you can find in a thesaurus without knowing its true meaning or part of speech.

    Example: What an amalgamation error! Mom thought Dad was picking me up from school.

    Better: What a mix-up! Mom thought Dad was picking me up from school.

Jargon or Technical Language—sophisticated words and phrases that don't match the audience you're addressing

Language like this can make your writing unnecessarily hard to follow—and can put off your reader. Use it only if it enhances clarity and provides examples or definitions that make sense for the audience.

    Example: The fall from my bicycle resulted in a hematoma on my knee.

    Better: I got a bruise on my knee from falling off my bike.

Wordiness—several words when fewer would do

This often happens when you're trying to sound smart. Unfortunately, it just makes your writing harder to read.

    Example: In the process of cleaning his room, Marco came across the handheld game he had lost earlier.

    Better: While cleaning his room, Marco found his handheld game.

Clichés—phrases that are so commonplace they've lost meaning and punch

    Example: Trying out for the soccer team? I'm still up in the air about it.

    Better: Trying out for the soccer team? I still haven't decided.

R.A.F.T.S. 14

You are a radio host. You are holding a contest for a pair of tickets to an upcoming sold-out concert by pop star Munki. Write an announcement to deliver on air, describing the contest and the prize and providing listeners with the necessary instructions (phone number, prompt song, and approximate time). The contest needs to be simple but fun. The explanation should be precise. Choose specific and accurate words so that listeners get it on the first listen.

Role: radio host
Audience: listeners
Format: announcement
Topic: a contest to win a pair of tickets
Strong Verbs: deliver, describe, provide

Write your announcement on a separate sheet of paper. Before you begin to write, jot down some details you might include.

Think About

- Have I used nouns and modifiers that help readers see a picture?

- Did I avoid using words that might confuse the reader?

- Did I try a new word and, if so, check to make sure I used it correctly?

- Are these the best words that can be used?

Jump Start Sheet

Days 1 and 3: My Unit Project To-Do List

- _____

- _____

- _____

- _____

Day 5: My Six-Word Statement on Strength

_____   _____   _____   _____   _____   _____

Focus on Word Study

Root: *geo*
Meaning: _____
Common Words That Contain the Root:

1.

2.

3.

My Wacky Word

_____

_____

_____

_____

_____

Write-On Sheet

Preview

Russell Freedman,

author of *The Adventures of Marco Polo*

Answer the questions below on your own or with a partner.

1. Russell Freedman prefers to be called a "factual author." Why do you think he might prefer this title over another, such as "nonfiction author"?

   _____

   _____

   _____

2. Freedman writes only about topics that interest him and that he is curious about. Why is this a good way to select topics?

   _____

   _____

   _____

3. Besides Marco Polo, Freedman has written about Eleanor Roosevelt, the Wright Brothers, and Crazy Horse. He enjoys writing about people in history who have strong characters. Who else is someone who fits that description? What would readers find interesting about him or her?

   _____

   _____

   _____

Bonus: Use the Internet to research another book that Russell Freedman has written. Write on note cards what you find out about it and share them with a classmate.

Freedom Counts

Think of a freedom that is important to you.
Then answer the questions below to help you
write a book page about it.

1. What is a freedom you value? Why is it important to you?

   _____

   _____

   _____

2. How would you define this freedom in your own words? Be sure to use
   specific and accurate words in your definition.

   _____

   _____

   _____

3. What does this freedom mean to you? Write a short story or anecdote
   about a time you exercised this freedom and felt lucky to have it.

   _____

   _____

   _____

4. Imagine you live in a country without this freedom. How would life be
   different? Give several examples to explain.

   _____

   _____

   _____

- Crafting Well-Built Sentences
- Varying Sentence Types
- **Capturing Smooth and Rhythmic Flow** • • • • • • • • • • • • • • • •
- Breaking the "Rules" to Create Fluency

Focus Mode: Expository
Theme: Strength

Sentence Fluency

Writing may seem like a silent act, but it isn't. When you read your drafts, listen for passages that sound smooth and rhythmic . . . and passages that don't. From there, revise. By doing that, you'll create sentence fluency— the music of language that makes your writing sound as good as it looks.

No doubt about it—I have fluency, but that eagle has *fly*-ency!

Capturing Smooth and Rhythmic Flow

Good writers revise sentences until they get them right. Their goal? Creating a piece that is so smooth and rhythmic it sounds musical. Good writers add, move, or remove words, then listen for how sentences sound individually and together. Create smooth-sounding sentences. Catch the rhythm of your writing.

Sentence Fluency

How is a piece of writing with smooth and rhythmic flow similar to a bird gliding through the air?

Rhythmic Reading

Fluent writing has a musical quality. When you read aloud any piece of writing, find the smooth and rhythmic flow, and go with it.

Here are some formats for your choral reading of "Valentine for Ernest Mann" by Naomi Shihab Nye. Choose one with your fellow group members.

1. Unison

Everyone in your group reads together at the same time.

2. Two groups

Divide your group into two. These smaller groups alternate stanzas.

3. Chorus

One group member reads the first line of each stanza. The other group members chime in on the other lines.

4. Word by Word

Each group member takes a turn reading a word.

5. Line by Line

Each group member takes a turn reading a line.

Once you've chosen a format, don't read like a robot. Pay attention to the words and what they mean . . . and then express yourself through the words. Here's how:

Switch your pitch.
Make your voice go up and down. Raise your pitch at the beginning of a line or sentence and lower it at the end (or raise it slightly if you are asking a question).

Adjust your rhythm.
Speed up for short sentences. Slow down for longer ones. Pause at commas, at the ends of lines, and at the ends of sentences.

Turn up your volume.
Emphasize important words by saying them a little bit louder.

Change your tone.
Use your voice to communicate just the right emotions—joy, sadness, wonder, and so forth.

R.A.F.T.S. 15

You are a TV reporter who normally covers fairly boring traffic events. But you have just been given a breakthrough chance at covering a major story: As you fly back to the station in the KIX15 skycopter, a high-speed chase erupts below you. As the sole reporter on the scene, you follow the chase as it unfolds, relaying a live report of the event back to the station. You notice that the getaway car is a very nice make and model, allowing the perpetrators to make smooth, almost rhythmic twists and turns. Make sure your summary of the event matches their driving style so that you convey the feeling as well as the details of the event to the public.

Role: TV traffic reporter
Audience: viewers
Format: live TV report
Topic: a high-speed chase
Strong Verbs: relay, convey

Write your TV report on a separate sheet of paper. Before you begin to write, jot down some details you might include.

Think About

- Is it easy to read the entire piece aloud?

- Do my sentences flow, one to the next?

- Do individual passages sound smooth when I read them aloud?

- Did I thoughtfully place different sentence types to enhance the main idea?

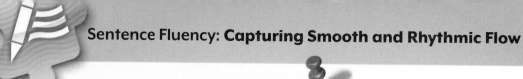

Jump Start Sheet

Days 1 and 3: My Unit Project To-Do List

- _____
- _____
- _____
- _____

Day 5: My Six-Word Statement on Strength

_____ _____ _____ _____ _____ _____

Focus on Grammar and Usage

Review your writing, find sentences in which you've used pronouns incorrectly, and revise two of those sentences here.

1. _____

_____

_____

_____

2. _____

_____

_____

_____

Write-On Sheet

Preview

Patricia C. McKissack, author of *A Picture of Freedom: The Diary of Clotee, a Slave Girl*

Answer the questions below on your own or with a partner.

1. Patricia McKissack worked as a teacher and an editor before becoming a writer. How do you think these careers helped her prepare to write books for young people?

_____

_____

_____

2. On many of her books, McKissack collaborates with her husband, Fred. How might working with a partner help make your writing better?

_____

_____

_____

3. Before writing a book, McKissack thinks through every detail. She says, "I can't work until I know where I'm going." What do you think she means?

_____

_____

_____

_____

Bonus: Find a book by Patricia McKissack or a passage from one of her books on the Internet, write down sentences that you find particularly fluent, and share them with a classmate.

Rhythm Check

Read aloud the excerpt from *A Picture of Freedom*. In the chart, write notes about how Patricia McKissack creates smooth and rhythmic flow.

Down below, let McKissack know how much you like her sentence flow!

Sentence Fluency

Sentence Lengths	Beginnings and Endings	The Sounds of Words and Phrases Within the Sentence

Discuss your notes with a partner. Then transform your thoughts into an e-mail to Patricia McKissack, explaining what makes her writing so fluent.

_____

_____

_____

_____

_____

Expository Publishing Checklist

Think you are ready to go public with your expository unit project? Use this form to make sure you've covered all the writing bases.

You've done an unconventionally good job!

Conventions

I remembered to

☐ include intriguing and accurate facts that came from reliable sources.

☐ weave in details that go beyond the obvious and show how much I know about my topic.

☐ choose a text structure that supports my big idea and makes my message clear.

☐ anticipate and answer readers' questions and help them make personal connections.

☐ develop the topic logically from beginning to end.

☐ use a compelling voice that expresses my fascination for the topic.

☐ explain any unusual words, phrases, or concepts.

☐ read my piece aloud to check how it will sound to the reader.

☐ proofread my piece carefully and clean up problems with conventions.

The purpose of my piece is

_____

The part that works the best is

_____

What I hope readers will take away from my piece is

_____

Focus Mode: Narrative

Throughout human history, people have been telling stories to make sense of the world. When you write in the narrative mode, you tell a story—either a made-up one (fiction) or a real one (nonfiction). Your stories should include characters, a setting, a timeline, and a problem and its solution. Along the way, they may include a surprise or two. And they should always capture your reader's interest and hang on to it, right to the end.

- Finding a Topic
- Focusing the Topic
- Developing the Topic
- **Using Details** ....

Focus Mode: Narrative
Theme: Truth

Ideas

Ideas are your central message—the main thoughts you want to share. To make your ideas strong, choose a topic you care about and focus on one interesting aspect of it. From there, weave in original and unexpected details to open your readers' eyes and show them something they might otherwise overlook.

Using Details

Vivid, accurate details take your work from *ho-hum* to *how about that!* You draw the reader in by describing how things look, taste, feel, sound, and smell. Stretching, for example, to find a little-known fact or to create a complex character puts readers in the moment with you—and once they get a taste of what you have to say, they'll hang on to your every word.

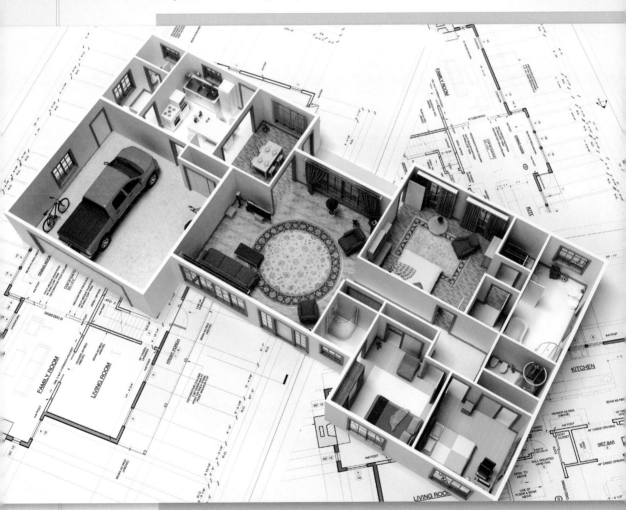

How is planning every inch of a building like using details in writing?

Home In on the Details

Details help the reader create mental images, focus on the topic, and hear the voice in a piece of writing. Here are some techniques for weaving details into your writing.

1. Saturate the Senses

Enable the reader to see, touch, taste, smell, and hear what's going on.

Example: The young alligator was about 18 inches long. Its greenish-gray skin was cool and smooth, not at all slimy. It smelled faintly salty. I heard the murmurs of admiration from the other tourists as I held it at arm's length.

2. Crystallize the Concept

Stick to your main idea and use details to support it.

Example: Korean kimchi has a tangy-salty-spicy-sour taste. A mixture of chili powder, salted shrimp, garlic, onion, and ginger root is liberally slathered on layers of cabbage or other vegetables, and then fermented.

3. Produce a Picture

Use specific words and phrases to create vivid images in the reader's mind.

Example: Hiking at Bryce Canyon, I felt dwarfed by the immense hoodoos. The 10- to 150-foot-tall rocky spires are mostly reddish brown with rainbow tints. Some stand alone. Others cluster like petrified giants.

4. Aim for Accuracy

Get the facts right. Provide believable details that enlighten the reader and invite him or her to bring knowledge and experience to the piece.

Example: The Conestoga wagons used by the pioneers were approximately the size of a current-day minivan. Imagine cramming all of your possessions into a space that's about 16 feet long, 4 feet high, and 4 feet deep!

5. Outdo the Obvious

Dig a little deeper. Research uncommon or little-known details.

Example: You know the Aztecs and Mayans drank chocolate. But did you know they also used cacao beans as currency? And when Cortez introduced chocolate to the Spanish, it was considered nutritious and medicinal.

R.A.F.T.S. 16

You are an amateur filmmaker creating a documentary about a little-known local animal—the whamscram—that gets its name from the deafeningly loud sound it makes to distract predators so that it can zip away with lightning speed. The whamscram interests you because it looks different to every person who sees it. After your first sighting, you decide to create a documentary movie of all the different descriptions witnesses have reported. Write the opening narration for the film, detailing how the whamscram looked to you (glow-in-the-dark fur; fuzzy teeth; large, spoon-shaped feet, for example), and the sound it made as it scrammed. Since you'll post the film online for whamscram lovers, the details about what you saw need to be specific, so that viewers can picture it precisely in their minds.

Role: amateur filmmaker
Audience: whamscram lovers
Format: documentary opening narration
Topic: whamscram appearance(s) and sound
Strong Verbs: create, record, report

Write your opening narration on a separate sheet of paper. Before you begin to write, jot down some details you might include.

Think About

- Did I create a picture in the reader's mind?

- Did I use details that draw upon the five senses (sight, touch, taste, smell, hearing)?

- Do my details stay on the main topic?

- Did I stretch for details beyond the obvious?

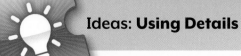

Ideas: Using Details

Jump Start Sheet

Unit Project Topic: _____

Days 1 and 3: My Unit Project To-Do List

- _____

- _____

- _____

- _____

Day 5: My Six-Word Statement on Truth

_____ _____ _____ _____ _____ _____

Focus on Word Study

Root: *socio*

Meaning: _____

Common Words That Contain the Root:

1.

2.

3.

My Wacky Word

_____

_____

_____

_____

Write-On Sheet

Ideas: Using Details

Preview

Steven Otfinoski, author of *Mythlopedia: All in the Family! A Look-It-Up Guide to the In-laws, Outlaws, and Offspring of Mythology*

Answer the questions below, on your own or with a partner.

1. Read the title of the mentor text. What details about the book's content and format does it provide?

   _____

   _____

   _____

   _____

2. What kind of details on mythological figures might Steven Otfinoski include to focus the topic and help the reader create mental images?

   _____

   _____

   _____

3. Otfinoski has also written *Coin Collecting for Kids, Hedgehogs and Other Insectivores, Latinos in the Arts,* and *Stan Lee: Comic Book Genius.* Which sounds like a book you'd like to read? What appeals to you from the title?

   _____

   _____

   _____

Bonus: Use the Internet to find out more about Steven Otfinoski. Write your findings on note cards and share them with a classmate.

Detailopedia

Answer the questions about Steven Otfinoski's use of details in *All in the Family*!

Forget King Midas. When it comes to using details, YOU have the golden touch!

Idea

1. Give one example of sensory imagery from the mentor text. Which of the senses does it relate to?

   _____

   _____

2. Otfinoski's main idea here is the fate of King Midas. Can you name some details that support it?

   _____

   _____

3. What are some new details you could add to bring your own knowledge and/or experience to the passage?

   _____

   _____

4. What detail(s) about Greek mythology did you learn from this passage?

   _____

   _____

Bonus:

Draw a picture of an image this excerpt created in your mind.

- Creating the Lead
- Using Sequence Words and Transition Words
- Structuring the Body
- **Ending With a Sense of Resolution**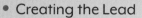

Focus Mode: Narrative
Theme: Truth

Organization

Organization is about how your idea unfolds from beginning to end— how you structure and arrange your details. An organized piece begins engagingly, moves along logically, and ends satisfyingly. You give readers the right amount of information at the right moments. When your organization is working, following the idea is effortless.

Ending With a Sense of Resolution

The ending is your last contact with readers—your opportunity to make them say, "Ah, yes," not "Huh?!" A good ending ties up the loose ends and answers any remaining questions. It sums up your thinking in a natural, thoughtful, and convincing way, and leaves readers with a sense of closure.

How is celebrating the final day of the year like ending a piece of writing with a sense of resolution?

That's a Wrap

There are many ways to wrap up a piece of narrative writing—and leave the reader satisfied. Here are a few for you to try.

1. Epiphany

Offer a sudden insight by the main character.

Example: Destiny turned to her friends with disgust. "Fine," she announced. "Go ahead without me. If you can't accept me for who I am, then I'm better off on my own."

2. Tragedy

End on a dark note to hammer home the gravity of the situation.

Example: It was all too much for Hachiro. He locked the door to the house for the last time, realizing as he did so that he might also be locking the door to the life he had always known.

3. Irony

Reveal an incongruity between what the main character says and does and how the story turns out.

Example: It happened often now that he was more sure about himself when he obeyed that urge to be honest and not hold back. Funny, he thought, a year ago I never would have hesitated to "little-white-lie" my way through anything.

4. Image

Hearken back to a key point in the story with a visual description.

Example: Arianna looked out the airplane window for a last glance at the lake, the buildings, and the mountains she loved.

5. Surprise

Conclude with a twist or unexpected turn of events.

Example: The judge gasped as he realized that the man he had just sentenced to life imprisonment was his own long-lost brother.

6. Hollywood Ending

Tie it up with a bow—make everyone happy, everything perfect.

Example: Cinderella and Prince Charming lived happily ever after . . . no, really. They did!

R.A.F.T.S. 17

Chillin'—that's the topic for your next Web article for *Teen Travel* magazine. As a travel writer/blogger, you've spent lots of time rushing from place to place in a hurry to get the next story—which means you know *all* the best places to relax. You want to share your know-how with the world. Pick your favorite location and tell the story of how you discovered just how truly perfect it is. Be sure to end with the same sense of smooth serenity you want your readers to feel about the place you're describing.

Role: travel blogger
Audience: teens
Format: online article
Topic: best places to relax
Strong Verbs: share, tell

Write your online article on a separate sheet of paper. Before you begin to write, jot down some details you might include.

Think About

- Have I wrapped up all the loose ends?
- Have I ended at the best place?
- Do I have an ending that makes my writing feel finished?
- Did I leave the reader with something to think about?

Jump Start Sheet

Days 1 and 3: My Unit Project To-Do List

- _____
- _____
- _____
- _____

Day 5: My Six-Word Statement on Truth

_____   _____   _____   _____   _____   _____

Focus on Grammar and Usage

Review your writing, find sentences in which you've used possessive pronouns incorrectly, and revise two of those sentences here.

1. _____

   _____

   _____

   _____

2. _____

   _____

   _____

   _____

Write-On Sheet

Preview

Richard Peck, author of
A Long Way From Chicago

Answer the questions below on your own or with a partner.

1. Richard Peck has said that he got his first glimpse of the world from reading books. What lasting glimpses of the world have you also gotten from books?

   _____

   _____

2. Once a high school teacher, Peck is grateful to his students for teaching him that "a novel must entertain first," before it can do anything else, a realization that has had a huge impact on his career. Do you agree—or disagree—with it? Why?

   _____

   _____

3. What does the phrase "A long way from . . ." imply about the importance of setting to Peck?

   _____

   _____

4. Peck has also written *Strays Like Us, Something for Joey,* and *A Year Down Yonder.* Which of these books would you most like to read? What is it about the title that intrigues you?

   _____

   _____

Bonus: Use the Internet to find out more about Richard Peck and his books. Write your findings on note cards and share them with a classmate.

Ending Like a Pro

Answer the questions about the ending of Richard Peck's prologue to *A Long Way From Chicago*. Then try your hand at writing a prologue to a collection of stories about your life.

The ending of a prologue concludes the beginning and introduces the middle . . . or is it the beginning? Now I'm confused!

1. Which type of ending does Richard Peck use—epiphany, tragedy, irony, image, surprise, or Hollywood ending?

_____

_____

2. What clues in the text helped you choose that type of ending?

_____

_____

3. How does the ending give you a sense of resolution?

_____

_____

4. How does the ending of the prologue set up the rest of the book—or make you want to keep reading?

_____

_____

Now it's your turn. Think about your life and what a collection about it might include. Stories from one summer or one school year? Stories that span several years? On the lines below, make notes about the collection. Then write its prologue on a separate sheet. Give it a fitting ending.

_____

_____

_____

- Establishing a Tone
- Conveying the Purpose
- Creating a Connection to the Audience
- **Taking Risks to Create Voice** • • • • • • • • • • • • • • • • • • •

Focus Mode: Narrative
Theme: Truth

Voice

Voice is the energy and attitude of a piece of writing. In fiction, voice can take on almost any tone, from humorous or hopeful to serious or somber. In nonfiction, it is often compelling, authoritative, and knowledgeable. You arrive at the right voice for a piece by thinking deeply about your purpose and audience for it. You "speak" in a way that connects to your audience.

My advice? Take risks with your writing—not with your hair!

Taking Risks to Create Voice

If you want to break away from bland, "voice-less" writing, you'll have to take some risks. You may have to tackle topics or use words and phrases that are new to you. This may feel uncomfortable at first, but with practice, it will feel natural. You'll find that taking risks leads to writing that is truly your own.

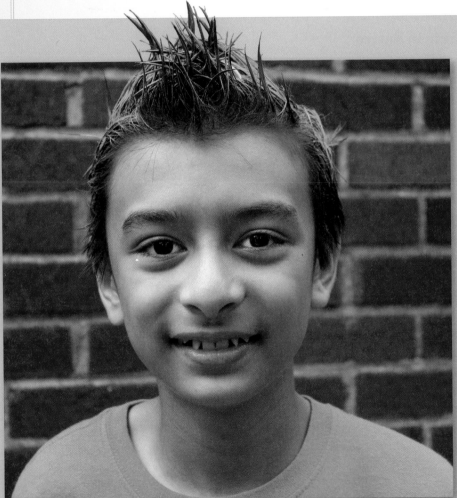

How is choosing a bold hairstyle like taking risks to create voice in writing?

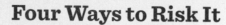

Four Ways to Risk It

Does that little judge looking over your shoulder keep telling you to play it safe in your writing? Sometimes you need to be risky to be yourself. Boot the judge and try these techniques.

1. Own the Words and Phrases

Stick your neck out! Find a new and different way to say something. Use unusual, distinctive, out-of-the ordinary words and phrases.

Example: How was my first singing lesson? It was a rhapsody in disaster. Even though I tried my best, I couldn't hit a single note.

2. Sprinkle in Satire

Use irony, sarcasm, or ridicule to make a point. But don't be hurtful or go overboard. A little bit of satire goes a long way.

Examples: • Irony: Lily named her new Chihuahua "Mega Dog."

• Sarcasm: "Hmm," said Rhea, looking at the charred French fries. "I suppose we could use these for a game of pick-up sticks."

• Ridicule: As he loomed over me, Rufus, the school bully, grunted that he was a grizzly in disguise. "Well. You certainly have the breath," I told him, "but I'm pretty sure my stuffed teddy, Norman, has sharper teeth."

3. Relate to the Reader

Maintain interest by putting yourself in your reader's position. Connect your ideas and experiences to those of your audience.

Example: Ever have a day when no one noticed your hard work or gave you credit for your efforts? The next time that happens, have your own "I Appreciate Me" Day.

4. Cause a Commotion

Make your readers laugh or cry. Prod them to shout out loud in agreement or disagreement. Get them pumped up and feeling something.

Example: Why should we let a bunch of health nuts tell us what we can and can't eat and drink? Don't let them take away the soda and snack machines at the rec center. All we'll have left is water and carrot sticks.

R.A.F.T.S. 18

An astronaut accidentally travels through a wormhole and appears in the year 3030. Picked up by a historian who speaks a little of the ancient "Ingallisk" language, the astronaut discovers that the people of 3030 have gotten history all mixed up: they believe that "Kris Topper Columbo" "selled the ocean blew" in a safety contraption called a "die-no soar," that "Shakes Spear" was a great warrior who helped win the "Regulatory War," that "French friers" were monks who catered royal parties, and so on. The historian is eager to learn the truth, so he asks the astronaut for an accurate account of one event he's most curious about. Write a dialogue of the conversation between the historian and the astronaut about an important historical event of your choice. Remember that the two don't speak quite the same "Ingallisk," so both characters will need to take risks with their words and gestures in order to understand each other.

Role: astronaut and historian from 3030
Audience: astronaut and historian from 3030
Format: dialogue
Topic: accurate account of a historic event
Strong Verbs: ask, discuss, account

Write your dialogue on a separate sheet of paper. Before you begin to write, jot down some details you might include.

Think About

- Have I used words that are not ordinary?
- Is my writing interesting, fresh, and original?
- Have I tried to make my writing sound like me?
- Have I tried something different from what I've done before?

Jump Start Sheet

Days 1 and 3: My Unit Project To-Do List

- _____
- _____
- _____
- _____

Day 5: My Six-Word Statement on Truth

_____ _____ _____ _____ _____ _____

Focus on Word Study

Root: *polis*
Meaning: _____
Common Words That Contain the Root:

1.
2.
3.

My Wacky Word

_____

_____

_____

_____

_____

Write-On Sheet

Preview

A Songwriter

Answer the questions below, on your own or with a partner.

1. How do you think songwriters find ideas for lyrics?

   _____

   _____

   _____

   _____

2. Do you think songwriters take risks to create voice in their lyrics? Back up your opinion with a song you know.

   _____

   _____

   _____

   _____

3. In what way are songwriters like story writers? In what way are they different?

   _____

   _____

   _____

   _____

Bonus: Look up on the Internet what a songwriter does. Write your findings on note cards and share them with a classmate.

Voice Those Lyrics

Find a partner and answer these questions about "Ballad of a Teenage Queen."

> How about "Ballad of a Teenage Trait Mate"? We're always breaking up and getting back together.

1. What can you say about the words and phrases in the lyrics? Are they striking? Or are they everyday words used well? Give some examples.

   _____

   _____

2. Did the songwriter use satire (the gentle use of irony, sarcasm, or ridicule) in the lyrics? How does the inclusion or lack of it affect voice in this song?

   _____

   _____

3. How do you connect to the lyrics as listener and reader?

   _____

   _____

4. What do you feel when you read or hear the lyrics? What lines touch your emotions? If you have listened to a recording of the song, what feelings did the melody evoke?

   _____

   _____

Extend the song by writing a new final stanza about what happens when the girl returns home and tries to reconnect with the boy. Capture the voice and follow the rhyme scheme established at the start of the song.

_____

_____

_____

_____

Narrative Publishing Checklist

Think you are ready to go public with your narrative unit project? Use this form to make sure you've covered all the writing bases.

You're so good, I'm speechless.

I remembered to

☐ present a clear, well-developed story line.

☐ include fascinating characters that grow and change over time.

☐ convey time and setting that make sense for the story.

☐ entertain, surprise, and challenge the reader.

☐ develop the story chronologically or take a risk and try a structure that also helps the reader follow the story easily.

☐ use an active voice to engage the reader.

☐ choose words that fit the characters, time, and place.

☐ read my piece aloud to check for places where I should speed up or slow down.

☐ proofread my piece carefully and clean up problems with conventions.

The purpose of my piece is

_____

My favorite part is

_____

What I hope readers will find most memorable about my piece is

_____

All

Focus Mode: Persuasive

If you want to be heard, it's important to know how to construct an argument. When you write in the persuasive mode, you write to convince the reader to agree with—or at least respect—your opinion on a topic of importance to you. You should clearly state your topic and position at the beginning and, from there, defend your position, using solid facts, undeniable evidence, and a confident tone.

- Applying Strong Verbs
- Selecting Striking Words and Phrases
- Using Specific and Accurate Words
- **Choosing Words That Deepen Meaning** ·

Focus Mode: Persuasive
Theme: Power

Word Choice

Words are the building blocks of writing. Well-chosen words bring your ideas into focus. They create images, spark the imagination, and grab the reader's attention. Word choice is verbal alchemy; it's how writers transform the ordinary into the extraordinary. Choose words that move, enlighten, and inspire.

Choosing Words That Deepen Meaning

I'll be right back. I've got sand in my swimsuit.

Word Choice

Good writers know that the first words that come to mind are rarely the ones they wind up using. They take time to think about words and move them around in their drafts. Replacing dull, common words with exciting, original ones helps you express exactly what you want to say in your writing.

How is taking a perfect picture like choosing words that deepen meaning?

Playing With Words

Word choice isn't all work and no play. Here are some figurative wordplay techniques that you can use to deepen the meaning and lighten up the tone of your writing. Read the definitions and examples, then try writing one of each on your own.

Idiom—a saying that has a meaning other than the literal definition

Example: *take a load off my mind*

My Example: _____

_____

Hyperbole—a word or phrase that is outrageously exaggerated

Example: *He told so many lies that if you stacked them up they would reach the moon.*

My Example: _____

_____

Oxymoron—an expression that combines two contradictory terms or ideas

Example: *jumbo shrimp; second best; small crowd*

My Example: _____

_____

Personification—a statement that gives human characteristics to an animal or object

Example: *My laptop hates me.*

My Example: _____

_____

Euphemism—a mild, indirect, or vague term that is used in place of a blunt, unpleasant, or offensive one

Example: *passed away* instead of *died*; *tells it like it is* instead of *rude*

My Example: _____

_____

R.A.F.T.S. 19

Upon the untimely death of their fearless leader, Moongape the wolf, in a tragic conflict of interest with a waterfall, the forest animals have congregated to elect a new sovereign. The top two contenders are Lightstep the mountain lion, who claims to be most deserving of power because a lion is the stealthiest, swiftest, and deadliest creature in the forest; and Darkwit the crow, who argues that cunning and the power of the mind trump physical strength. Choose one of the candidates and, from its point of view, write a pitch to the crowd, arguing in detail why you should be crowned instead of your opponent. This vote will determine the course of your life and the lives of all the animals that follow you—so word your pitch carefully to get across your full and true meaning.

Role: Lightstep the Lion or Darkwit the Crow
Audience: forest animals
Format: pitch for candidacy
Topic: why you should rule the forest
Strong Verbs: claim, pitch, argue

Write your pitch on a separate sheet of paper. Before you begin to write, jot down some details you might include.

Think About

- Did I choose words that show I really thought about them?
- Have I tried to use words without repeating myself?
- Do my words capture the reader's imagination?
- Have I found the best way to express myself?

Word Choice: **Choosing Words That Deepen Meaning**

Jump Start Sheet

Unit Project Topic: _____

Days 1 and 3: My Unit Project To-Do List

- _____

- _____

- _____

- _____

Day 5: My Six-Word Statement on Power

_____   _____   _____   _____   _____   _____

Focus on Grammar and Usage

Review your writing, find sentences in which you've used the wrong comparative adjective and/or used the passive voice, and revise two of those sentences here.

1. _____

_____

_____

_____

2. _____

_____

_____

_____

Write-On Sheet

Word Choice: **Choosing Words That Deepen Meaning**

Preview

Ben Hillman, author of *How Strong Is It?*

Answer the questions below, on your own or with a partner.

1. In addition to being an author and illustrator, Ben Hillman is an animator and filmmaker. How do you think making movies and writing books might be similar?

_____

_____

_____

_____

2. Other titles in Hillman's "How" series are *How Fast Is It?*, *How Big Is It?*, and *How Weird Is It?* Can you suggest another title for the series and explain its main idea?

_____

_____

_____

_____

3. Ben Hillman's books have been described as "mind bending" and "so freaking cool." What does that suggest he might be like as a person?

_____

_____

_____

_____

Bonus: Look on the Internet for books by Ben Hillman. Pick one you'd like to read and talk about it with a partner.

Stickier Than . . .

Super sticky glue . . . made from bacteria?
Who would buy that?! Write an ad to persuade consumers.

First, give the glue a catchy name:

_____

Replace each line of the famous Superman quote (below) with words and phrases that describe the glue.

Faster than a speeding bullet.
More powerful than a locomotive.
Able to leap tall buildings in a single bound!
Look! Up in the sky!
It's a bird!
It's a plane!
It's Superman!

Stickier than _____.

Stronger than _____.

Able to _____!
        (action verb)   (description of a location)

It's a _____!

It's a _____!

It's _____!
                (name of your glue)

Now, write an advertisement for the glue on a separate sheet of paper. Be sure to include a picture of the product—bottle, tube, stick, or jar with label.

- Crafting Well-Built Sentences
- Varying Sentence Types
- Capturing Smooth and Rhythmic Flow
- **Breaking the "Rules" to Create Fluency** ·

Focus Mode: Persuasive
Theme: Power

Sentence Fluency

Writing may seem like a silent act, but it isn't. When you read your drafts, listen for passages that sound smooth and rhythmic . . . and passages that don't. From there, revise. By doing that, you'll create sentence fluency—the music of language that makes your writing sound as good as it looks.

Breaking the "Rules" to Create Fluency

I'll unleash my creativity. But, tell me, who unleashed the ducks?

Following grammar rules makes your writing understandable, but not always engaging. Sometimes you have to break the rules to energize your writing. Use sentence fragments to make a point. Start a sentence or two with a conjunction. Write the way you talk. Surprise your reader. Unleash your creativity.

How is breaking the "rules" to create fluency like taking an unplanned detour for an unexpected event?

Special Effects

When you bend or break rules purposefully in writing, you create spectacular, memorable moments, like special effects in movies.

Here are some rules about sentences that writers sometimes choose to deliberately break:

Rule: Always write in complete sentences, not fragments.

Writers often use fragments to make readers sit up and take notice.

Example: Saturday morning. My favorite time of my favorite day of the week. I rolled over, pulled the covers over my head, and went back to sleep. Ah, yes.

Rule: Never repeat words and phrases.

Never say *never*. Repetition can add emphasis and rhythm to writing.

Example: Study, study, study. All Sami seemed to do anymore was study.

Rule: Remove all run-ons.

People don't always pause when they speak. Run-on sentences can capture the energy and rhythm of natural speech.

Example: "I'm not gonna stop, can't give up, gotta make it, gonna win." Julio panted these words over and over as he ran toward the finish line.

Rule: Don't ever start a sentence with a conjunction.

But sometimes it's okay. Starting with a conjunction can enhance flow by connecting thoughts immediately.

Example: It was going to be hot, too hot for daily doubles or a scrimmage after school. And it was going to storm later in the afternoon. But we didn't care. And it didn't rain after all. Or at least not very much.

Choose one example to rewrite below. Your challenge: Fix the broken rule. Use correct English. Then discuss with a partner how your changes affect the example's sentence fluency.

_____

_____

_____

_____

R.A.F.T.S. 20

You're a famous vocal artist; everything you say or do gets attention. A strong believer in the power of the word to create change, you've decided to write a song (or rap) to promote a cause (social, environmental, political) that you deeply believe in. One of the most important elements of catchy lyrics is rhythm and fluency, so be sure to use the rules of grammar in just the right way (including bending and breaking them when necessary) to communicate to your faithful fans a message that is both poignant and memorable.

Role: famous vocal artist
Audience: your fan base
Format: song or rap lyrics
Topic: a cause that is important to you
Strong Verbs: believe, create change, promote

Write your lyrics on a separate sheet of paper. Before you begin to write, jot down some details you might include.

Think About

- Did I use fragments with style and purpose?
- Do I begin a sentence informally to create a conversational tone?
- Does my dialogue sound authentic?
- Did I try weaving in exclamations and single words to add emphasis?

Jump Start Sheet

Days 1 and 3: My Unit Project To-Do List

- _____

- _____

- _____

- _____

Day 5: My Six-Word Statement on Power

_____ _____ _____ _____ _____ _____

Focus on Word Study

Root: *loc*
Meaning: _____
Common Words That Contain the Root:

1.

2.

3.

My Wacky Word

_____

_____

_____

_____

_____

Write-On Sheet

Sentence Fluency: Breaking the "Rules" to Create Fluency

Preview

A Public Speaker

Answer the questions below, on your own or with a partner.

1. A public speaker can gain fame for his or her speeches. Name a speech you've heard of and liked. What was it about? What ideas did it promote?

_____

_____

_____

_____

2. Name a time and place at which you might give a speech. Do you think it would be fun or do you quake at the very thought of it? What is a topic you might choose?

_____

_____

_____

_____

3. What do you think makes a public speaker effective? What does he or she say or do that makes you want to keep listening?

_____

_____

_____

_____

Bonus: Look up on the Internet what a public speaker does. Write your findings on note cards and share them with a classmate.

Sound Off

Fill in the chart to brainstorm ideas for your Sound Off speech.

Sound off? Gladly. I've got a lot to get off my chest.

Sentence Fluency

What I Want Adults to Know	Why It's Important	Action I Hope Adults Will Take

1. Which idea do you feel most strongly about? What are some examples you could use to make your position clear in your speech?

_____

_____

_____

_____

2. Think about the tone Adora Svitak used in her speech. What tone(s) will you use?

_____

_____

_____

3. What are some key points you want to make in your speech?

_____

_____

_____

_____

- Ideas
- Organization
- Voice
- Word Choice
- Sentence Fluency
- Conventions
- Presentation

Focus Mode:
Persuasive

Theme:
Power

All Traits

Whether you're writing a persuasive piece about protecting a local wilderness area, an expository piece comparing ancient deities, or a narrative piece about learning to snowboard—and spraining your wrist, you must be skilled in all the traits in order to grab and hold your reader's attention.

Putting the Traits Together

All year, you have been reading your writing closely and breaking it down trait by trait. Now it's time to combine the traits and get them working together. You may be amazed at how much you have developed as a writer.

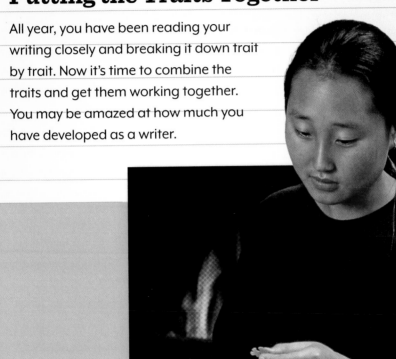

How is finishing a jigsaw puzzle like using all the traits in a piece of writing?

Trait Basics

All year, you've been learning about the traits and their key qualities. Now it's time to review what you know. For each trait, write a beginner's definition that would explain the trait to a kindergartner or a first grader, and tell why it's important in his or her writing.

1. Ideas

Definition: _____

Why it's important: _____

2. Organization

Definition: _____

Why it's important: _____

3. Voice

Definition: _____

Why it's important: _____

4. Word Choice

Definition: _____

Why it's important: _____

5. Sentence Fluency

Definition: _____

Why it's important: _____

6. Conventions

Definition: _____

Why it's important: _____

7. Presentation

Definition: _____

Why it's important: _____

R.A.F.T.S. 21

You're a marketer for Globahugs Intl, and you've just been handed the assignment of a lifetime: designing the packaging for their premier new product, Friend-in-a-Box—a portable companion who never gets tired of listening, playing sports, shopping, watching sappy (or scary) movies, lending you money, being there for you, studying, or displaying any of the qualities you most desire in a friend. The packaging should provide useful information, such as those friend-worthy qualities, as well as eye-catching logos and slogans that will convince consumers that they, too, would benefit from a friend . . . in a box. Maximize your persuasive power by combining everything you've learned about the traits.

Role: marketer
Audience: consumers worldwide
Format: product packaging
Topic: Friend-in-a-Box
Strong Verbs: design, convince, maximize, combine

Write your product packaging information on a separate sheet of paper. Before you begin to write, jot down some details you might include.

Think About

- Is my topic focused and manageable?
- Does my idea unfold logically?
- Have I engaged the reader and used an appropriate tone?
- Are my words and phrases accurate, yet do they spark the imagination?
- Are my sentences solid, varied, and smooth?

Jump Start **Sheet**

Days 1 and 3: My Unit Project To-Do List

- _____
- _____
- _____
- _____

Day 5: My Six-Word Statement on Power

_____ _____ _____ _____ _____ _____

Focus on Grammar and Usage

Review your writing, find sentences in which you've incorrectly used adverbs and irregular verbs, and rewrite the sentences here.

1. _____

   _____

   _____

   _____

2. _____

   _____

   _____

   _____

Write-On Sheet

Blue Balliett, author of *The Danger Box*

Answer the questions below, on your own or with a partner.

1. Blue Balliett grew up in New York City. How might growing up in a big city have influenced her ability to write believably about a wide variety of characters?

_____

_____

_____

_____

2. Every crowded train or bus is full of stories—that's Blue Balliett's belief. What is a story idea from your walk or ride to school today?

_____

_____

_____

_____

3. Blue Balliett is intrigued by the idea that physical disabilities can allow people to accomplish things that others might not. What do you think she means by that? Can you give an example?

_____

_____

_____

Bonus: Look on the Internet for information about Blue Balliett. Share with a classmate one interesting fact that you learn.

My Unique Traits

Fill in the web with your personal traits. Include interests, talents, likes, and dislikes. Then list one pro and one con for each trait.

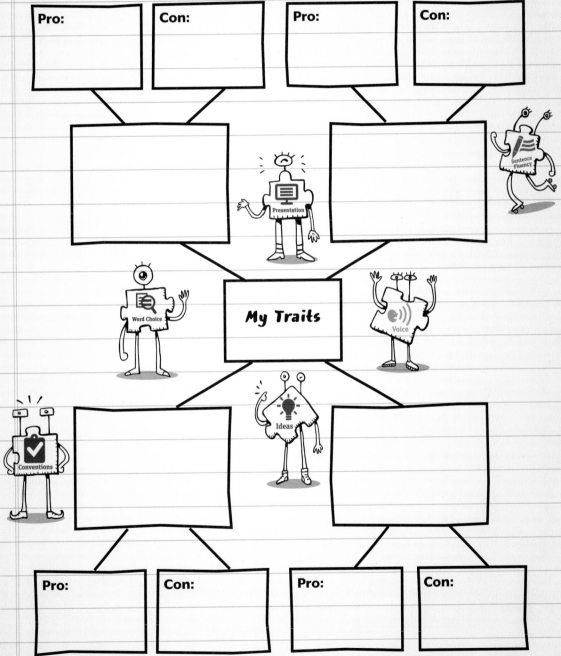

Pro:

Con:

Pro:

Con:

My Traits

Pro:

Con:

Pro:

Con:

Persuasive Publishing Checklist

Think you are ready to go public with your persuasive unit project? Use this form to make sure you've covered all the writing bases.

I remembered to

☐ state my position on the topic clearly and stick with it.

☐ offer good, sound reasoning that the reader can relate to easily.

☐ provide solid facts, opinions, and examples that are based on reliable, objective sources.

☐ expose weaknesses in other positions.

☐ develop my argument using solid reasoning from beginning to end.

☐ use a compelling, confident voice to add credibility.

☐ explain any unusual words, phrases, or concepts.

☐ read my piece aloud to check how it will sound to the reader.

☐ proofread my piece carefully and clean up problems with conventions.

The purpose of my piece is

_____

The most critical point I make is

_____

What I hope readers will take away from my piece is

_____

You've persuaded me. In fact, your project is persuasive perfection!

Conventions

Week

1

Looking Back on Myself as a Writer

Week

2

Writing as Experts

Week

3

Fun Writing-Related Activities

Week

4

More Writing-Related Activities

Wrapping Up the Year

As the writing year draws to a close, let's look back at what you've learned about writing and how the traits have helped you improve. We'll stop to enjoy what you've written, look ahead to next year, and, while we're at it, have some fun.

The beginning of the school year . . . that was a while back, wasn't it? To get from there to here, you've spent lots of time writing and learning about writing. Now it's time to wrap up the writing year. This week, you will

1 create a practical guide to writing called *Getting Writing Right* that sums up what you've learned this year about the writing traits.

2 write and produce a video introducing yourself to next year's writing teacher. You'll include details about how you've grown as a writer, and what you still need to work on.

Working It Out

On this sheet, capture what you've learned this year about your chosen trait—and why it's important. You'll use the information to write a section of a lighthearted, encouraging guide to writing called *Getting Writing Right*.

My Group's Trait: _____

What I Learned	Why It's Important

Writing on the Light Side

Use this sheet to plan your section of *Getting Writing Right*.

My Group's Trait: _____

What We Learned About It:

_____

_____

_____

Why It's Important:

_____

_____

_____

Our Lighthearted, Encouraging Spin on It:

_____

_____

_____

_____

Interesting Elements to Include in the Section (such as cartoon characters with speech bubbles, quotations from famous authors, or passages from mentor texts):

_____

_____

Let Me Introduce Myself

Who are you as a writer? What do you want your teacher for next year to know? Write about it here. You'll use the information to create a video for him or her.

1. My Name:

   _____

2. Types of Writing I Most Like to Do:

   _____

   _____

3. My Favorite Trait and Why I Like It:

   _____

   _____

4. My Greatest Strength as a Writer:

   _____

   _____

5. My Greatest Challenge as a Writer:

   _____

   _____

6. How I Hope to Improve My Writing Next Year:

   _____

   _____

> You always choose words that make us proud.

Word Choice

> And arrange them to sound good when we read them aloud.

Sentence Fluency

Think about all the writing you did this year—and all you've learned about writing, thanks to your efforts. It's time to take a close look at just how much you've grown and, from there, use your expertise to help next year's entering class. This week, you will

1 write a paper in the same mode and on the same general topic as your beginning-of-year benchmark paper. You'll reread the original and compare the two pieces to see what you've learned.

2 write a skit from the point of view of an expert in one of the traits—and perform the skit for the class.

3 clean out your writing folder.

Benchmark Paper Planner

Write the mode and topic of your beginning-of-year paper. Then use the space below to plan a new paper on the same topic and in the same mode. Feel free to make lists of key points, write guiding questions, create a graphic organizer, or do anything else that will help you organize your thoughts. When your brain says, "Enough planning!" start writing your draft on a separate sheet of paper.

Mode: _____   Topic: _____

Writing as Experts

Revision and Editing Reminders

Revising and editing can take a lot of time, so follow these steps to keep the process manageable.

1. **Reread your draft and think about**
   - adding and deleting information and making details specific and accurate.
   - checking the beginning and ending to make sure they work well.
   - using a tone that is appropriate for your audience and captures the right amount of energy.
   - eliminating repetitive words and phrases and replacing them with ones that are more unusual or original.
   - creating smooth and rhythmic flow by varying sentence beginnings, lengths, and types.

2. **Go ahead and revise your draft.**

3. **Now look at your piece with an editor's eye by**
   - checking spelling.
   - using correct punctuation.
   - inserting a paragraph break when introducing a new idea.
   - finding the right places to capitalize.
   - applying grammar and usage rules.

4. **Create a final piece for the reader.**

Trait Expert

Which trait do you know the most about? Write a one-minute, two-person skit in which you explain the trait to a new eighth grader. Use what you've learned this year to make the trait crystal clear to him or her.

The trait: _____

Things that are important to know about the trait:

_____

_____

_____

_____

_____

_____

_____

_____

_____

_____

_____

_____

_____

Use this information to write your skit on a separate sheet of paper.

Fun Writing-Related Activities

The end of the year is approaching, and you've done a lot of writing since it began. When you stop to think about it, you'll realize that what you've learned this year will last you the rest of your life—because writing is an essential skill, no matter where you go or what you do.

This week, the scale tips to the "fun" side of writing, with group activities that allow you to show what you know!

Puppet Show Planner

Lights, camera, action! It's time to plan your puppet show for young writers.

Trait: _____

Key Qualities of the Trait:

_____

_____

Important Points to Make in the Script:

_____

_____

My Puppet's Name: _____

Sketch your puppet here:

Use all of the above to help write your script on a separate sheet.

Acrostic Poem

In an acrostic poem, the first letter of each line spells out a word that captures the poem's main idea or theme. Here are two examples:

Variety for the reader.
Originality adds life.
Inspiration is important.
Connect to the audience.
Extend yourself and take a risk.

Information
Developed topic
Experiences
Accurate details
Story line

Choose a trait and draft an acrostic poem of your own on a separate sheet of paper. Copy your finished version onto a clean sheet.

Now it's definitely time to enter the no-assignment zone, kick back, and have some fun. You'll also want to review your remaining writing and take home the pieces that mean most to you, so you can read them in the years to come. And don't forget to give your teacher a helping hand in taking down bulletin boards, cleaning up the classroom, and storing materials for next year's class. After that, say so long to your classmates—and thank them for a great year of writing!

Please *Do* Play With Your Words

Hip, hip, hooray for word play, we say! Try these fun activities. But be careful—once you get started, it may be hard to stop!

Spoonerisms a twist of initial consonant sounds that radically changes the meaning of a phrase

Examples: "a crushing blow" to "a blushing crow"; "a well-oiled bicycle" to "a well-boiled icicle"

Your turn: _____

_____

Knock, Knock Jokes (You know the pattern.)

Example: **A**: Knock, knock.
                B: Who's there?
                A: Herb.
                B: Herb who?
                A: Herb you were looking for some fun and games!

Your turn: _____

_____

Hink Pinks riddles with answers made up of two rhyming words

Example: What is a library robber? A book crook!

Your turn: _____

_____

Pangrams sentences that contain all the letters of the alphabet

Example: The quick brown fox jumps over the lazy dog.

Your turn: _____

_____

Icononyms words with initial letters that capture their meaning visually

Examples: M for *mountain*; S for *snake*

Your turn: _____

_____

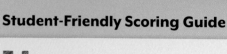

Ideas

the content of your piece—its central message and the details that support that message

6 EXPERT

HIGH

My topic is well developed and focused. My piece contains specific, interesting, and accurate details, and new thinking about this topic.

- I have a clear central theme or a simple, original story line.
- I've narrowed my theme or story line to create a focused piece that is a pleasure to read.
- I've included original information to support my main idea.
- I've included specific, interesting, and accurate details that will create pictures in the reader's mind.

5 WELL DONE

4 ALMOST THERE

MIDDLE

My piece includes many general observations about the topic, but lacks focus and clear, accurate details. I need to elaborate.

- I've stayed on the topic, but my theme or story line is too broad.
- I haven't dug into the topic in a logical, focused way.
- My unique perspective on this topic is not coming through as clearly as it could.
- The reader may have questions after reading this piece because my details leave some questions unanswered.

3 MAKING STRIDES

2 ON MY WAY

LOW

I'm still thinking about the theme or story line for this piece. So far, I've only explored possibilities.

- I've jotted down some ideas for topics, but it's a hodgepodge.
- Nothing in particular stands out as important in my piece.
- I have not written much. I may have only restated the assignment.
- My details are thin and need to be checked for accuracy.

1 GETTING STARTED

Organization

the internal structure of your piece—the thread of logic, the pattern of meaning

HIGH

6 EXPERT

My details unfold in a logical order. The structure makes reading my piece a breeze.

- My beginning grabs the reader's attention.
- I've used sequence and transition words to guide the reader.
- All of my details fit together logically and move along smoothly.
- My ending gives the reader a sense of closure and something to think about.

5 WELL DONE

MIDDLE

4 ALMOST THERE

My piece's organization is pretty basic and predictable. I have the three essential ingredients, a beginning, middle, and end, but that's about it.

- My beginning is clear, but unoriginal. I've used a technique that writers use all too often.
- I've used simple sequence and transition words that stand out too much.
- Details need to be added or moved around to create a more logical flow of ideas.
- My ending needs work; it's pretty canned.

3 MAKING STRIDES

2 ON MY WAY

LOW

My piece doesn't make much sense because I haven't figured out a way to organize it. The details are jumbled together at this point.

- My beginning doesn't indicate where I'm going or why I'm going there.
- I have not grouped ideas or connected them using sequence and transition words.
- With no sense of order, it will be a challenge for the reader to sort out how the details relate.
- I haven't figured out how to end this piece.

1 GETTING STARTED

Voice

the tone of the piece—your personal stamp, which is achieved through an understanding of purpose and audience

HIGH

6 EXPERT

I've come up with my own "take" on the topic. I had my audience and purpose clearly in mind as I wrote and presented my ideas in an original way.

- My piece is expressive, which shows how much I care about my topic.
- The purpose for this piece is clear, and I've used a tone that suits that purpose.
- There is no doubt in my mind that the reader will understand how I think and feel about my topic.
- I've expressed myself in some new, original ways.

5 WELL DONE

MIDDLE

4 ALMOST THERE

My feelings about the topic come across as uninspired and predictable. The piece is not all that expressive, nor does it reveal a commitment to the topic.

- In a few places, my authentic voice comes through, but only in a few.
- My purpose for writing this piece is unclear to me, so the tone feels "off."
- I've made little effort to connect with the reader; I'm playing it safe.
- This piece sounds like lots of others on this topic. It's not very original.

3 MAKING STRIDES

LOW

2 ON MY WAY

I haven't thought at all about my purpose or audience for the piece and, therefore, my voice falls flat. I'm pretty indifferent to the topic and it shows.

- I've put no energy into this piece.
- My purpose for writing this piece is a mystery to me, so I'm casting about aimlessly.
- Since my topic isn't interesting to me, chances are my piece won't be interesting to the reader. I haven't thought about my audience.
- I have taken no risks. There is no evidence that I find this topic interesting or care about it at all.

1 GETTING STARTED

Word Choice

the vocabulary you use to convey meaning and enlighten the reader

HIGH

6 EXPERT

The words and phrases I've selected are accurate, specific, and natural-sounding. My piece conveys precisely what I want to say, because of my powerful vocabulary.

- My piece contains strong verbs that bring it alive.
- I stretched by using the perfect words and phrases to convey my ideas.
- I've used content words and phrases with accuracy and precision.
- I've picked the best words and phrases, not just the first ones that came to mind.

5 WELL DONE

4 ALMOST THERE

MIDDLE

My words and phrases make sense but aren't very accurate, specific, or natural-sounding. The reader won't have trouble understanding them. However, he or she may find them uninspiring.

- I've used passive voice. I should rethink passages that contain passive voice and add "action words."
- I haven't come up with extraordinary ways to say ordinary things.
- My content words and phrases are accurate but general. I might have overused jargon. I need to choose words that are more precise.
- I need to revise this piece by replacing its weak words and phrases with strong ones.

3 MAKING STRIDES

2 ON MY WAY

LOW

My words and phrases are so unclear, the reader may wind up more confused than entertained, informed, or persuaded. I need to expand my vocabulary to improve this piece.

- My verbs are not strong. Passive voice permeates this piece.
- I've used bland words and phrases throughout—or the same words and phrases over and over.
- My content words are neither specific nor accurate enough to make the meaning clear.
- My words and phrases are not working; they distract the reader rather than guide him or her.

1 GETTING STARTED

Sentence Fluency

the way the text looks and sounds as it flows through your piece

6 EXPERT

HIGH

My piece is strong because I've written a variety of well-built sentences. I've woven those sentences together to create a smooth-sounding piece.

- I've constructed and connected my sentences for maximum impact.
- I've varied my sentence lengths and types—short and long, simple and complex.
- When I read my piece aloud, it is pleasing to my ear.
- I've broken grammar rules intentionally at points to create impact and interest.

5 WELL DONE

4 ALMOST THERE

MIDDLE

Although my sentences lack variety or creativity, most of them are grammatically correct. Some of them are smooth, while others are choppy and awkward.

- I've written solid shorter sentences. Now I need to try some longer ones.
- I've created different kinds of sentences, but the result is uneven.
- When I read my piece aloud, I stumble in a few places.
- Any sentences that break grammar rules are accidental and don't work well.

3 MAKING STRIDES

2 ON MY WAY

LOW

My sentences are choppy, incomplete, or rambling. I need to revise my piece extensively to make it more readable.

- Many of my sentences don't work because they're poorly constructed.
- I've used the same sentence lengths and types over and over again.
- When I read my piece aloud, I stumble in many places.
- If I've broken grammar rules, it's not for stylistic reasons—it's because I may not understand those rules.

1 GETTING STARTED

Conventions

the mechanical correctness of your piece, which helps guide the reader through the text

HIGH

6 EXPERT

My piece proves I can use a range of conventions with skill and creativity. It is ready for its intended audience.

- My spelling is strong. I've spelled all or nearly all the words accurately.
- I've used punctuation creatively and correctly and have begun new paragraphs in the right places.
- I've used capital letters correctly throughout my piece, even in tricky places.
- I've taken care to apply standard English grammar and usage.

5 WELL DONE

4 ALMOST THERE

MIDDLE

My writing still needs editing to correct problems in one or more conventions. I've stuck to the basics and haven't tried challenging conventions.

- I've misspelled words that I use all the time, as well as complex words that I don't use as often.
- My punctuation is basically strong, but I should review it one more time. I indented some of the paragraphs, but not all of them.
- I've correctly used capital letters in obvious places (such as the word *I*) but not in others.
- Even though my grammar and usage are not 100 percent correct, my audience should be able to read my piece.

3 MAKING STRIDES

2 ON MY WAY

LOW

The problems I'm having with conventions make this piece challenging to read, even for me! I've got lots of work to do before it's ready for its intended audience.

- Extensive spelling errors make my piece difficult to read and understand.
- I haven't punctuated or paragraphed the piece well, which makes it difficult for the reader to understand or enjoy my writing.
- My use of capital letters is so inconsistent, it's distracting.
- I need to clean up the piece considerably in terms of grammar and usage.

1 GETTING STARTED

Presentation

the physical appearance of your piece—the welcome mat that invites the reader in

6 EXPERT

HIGH

My piece's appearance makes it easy to read and enjoy. I've taken care to ensure that it is pleasing to my reader's eye.

- I've written clearly and legibly. My letters, words, and the spaces between them are uniform.

- My choice of font style, size, and/or color makes my piece a breeze to read.

- My margins frame the text nicely. There are no tears, smudges, or cross-outs.

- Text features such as bulleted lists, charts, pictures, and headers are working well.

5 WELL DONE

4 ALMOST THERE

MIDDLE

My piece still looks like a draft. Many visual elements should be cleaned up and handled with more care.

- My handwriting is readable, but my letters and words and the spaces between them should be treated more consistently.

- My choice of font style, size, and/or color seems "off"—inappropriate for my intended audience.

- My margins are uneven. There are some tears, smudges, or cross-outs.

- I've handled simple text features well but am struggling with the more complex ones.

3 MAKING STRIDES

2 ON MY WAY

LOW

My piece is almost unreadable because of its appearance. It's not ready for anyone but me to read.

- My handwriting is so hard to read, it creates a visual barrier.

- The font styles, sizes, and/or colors I've chosen are dizzying. They're not working.

- My margins are uneven or nonexistent, making the piece difficult to read.

- I haven't used text features well, even simple ones.

1 GETTING STARTED

Common Prefixes and Suffixes

Prefixes A prefix is a letter or group of letters added to the beginning of a root to change its meaning.

Prefix	Definition	Prefix	Definition
acro-	high, topmost, at the extremity	mis-	bad, badly, wrongly
ambi-, amphi-	both, around, about	mono-	one, alone, single
anti-	against, opposed to	multi-	many
auto-	self	neo-	new, young, recent, latest
bi-	two, twice, on two sides	non-	not, lacking, without
by-	near, side, secondary or incidental	ob-, oc-, of-	before, against, over
co-, col-, com-, con-, cor-	together with, joint, to the same degree	oct-, octa-, octo-	eight
de-	from, down, reverse the action	over-	upper, outer, superior, passing above, too much
deca-	ten	paleo-	ancient, early
deci-	one-tenth	pan-	all, every, universal
di-	two, double, twice; not, away from (see dis-)	para-	at the side of, in a secondary position
dia-	through, throughout, apart, between	penta-	five
dis-	not, opposite of, lack of, away from	per-	through, throughout, completely, very thoroughly
e-	out, beyond, away from, without	peri-	around, about, enclosing, near
em-, en-	put into or on, cover, make, subject to	poly-	many, much, excessive
endo-	within	post-	after, later
epi-	upon, over, on the outside	pre-	before, in front of, superior to
equa-, equi-	equal, equally	pro-	for, forward
ex- (w/hyphen)	former	proto-	first
ex-	out of, outside, from	pseudo-	false, deceptive
fore-	before, ahead of, front	quad-	four
hemi-	half	quint-	five
hetero-	different	re-	again, back, reverse
hex-, hexa-	six	self-	by oneself, within, automatic
homo-	same, equal to, like	sest-, sex-	six
il-, im-, in-, ir-	not, lack of	sub-	under, beneath, to a lesser degree, bordering
im-, in-	in, into, within	super-, supr-	above, beyond, over
inter-	between	syl-, sym-, syn-, sys-	with, together
intra-	within, inside	tele-	at, over, or from a distance, far away
macr-, macro-	large, long	tetra-	four
mal-	bad, badly, wrong, ill	trans-	across, beyond, over
mega-	very large, great, powerful	tri-	three
meta-	change in, after, going beyond or higher	un-	not, the opposite of
micro-	very small, minute	under-	beneath, below normal, too little
mid-	middle	uni-	one, only
mini-	small, brief		

Common Prefixes and Suffixes (continued)

Suffixes A suffix is a letter or group of letters added to the end of a root to form a new word. Adding a suffix often requires a spelling change to the root word.

Suffix	Definition	Suffix	Definition
-able, -ible	capable of, likely to, worthy of	-ish	having the characteristics of, native to
-al, -ial	of, related to, having the characteristics of	-ism	act of, state of, school of, system, manner
-ance, -ancy	state of, quality of, act of, process of	-ist	a person who, that which
-ant, -ent	someone who, agent of, performing the task of	-itis	disease, inflammation of, preoccupation with
-ar, -er, -or	someone who, something that, native of	-ity, -ty	state of, quality of being, instance of
-ary, -ory	relating to, having the qualities of, place where	-ive, -ative, -itive	causing, tending to do something
-asis, -esis, -osis	action, condition, process	-ize	make, cause to become, subject to, engage in
-ate	cause, make, provide or treat with	-less	without, not able to be
-cian, -ian	a person who practices or performs a skill	-like	similar to, resembling
-cide	kill, killing, killer	-ly	in the manner of, in the order of
-cy	action, function, rank, condition of being	-mania	exaggerated enthusiasm, uncontrollable desire
-dom	quality of, state of, realm of, power of	-ment	action of, process of, result of, degree of being
-ee	one who is receiving or performing an action	-meter	measure; device for measuring
-en	made of, added to	-ness	state of, quality of
-ence, -ency	state of, quality	-ology, -logy	study of, science of, branch of learning
-er	more than (compares two things); one that is or engages in some activity or profession	-or	one that does a specific thing
-ery	place to or for, practice of, product of, condition of	-ous, -eous, -ious	full of, having the qualities of
-ese	native of, language of	-phobia	fear, hatred
-est	most (compares three or more things)	-scope	an instrument for seeing
-ful	full of, having the quality of, able to cause	-ship	condition of, state of, quality of being, skill of
-fy	make	-tude	state of, condition of, instance of being
-hood	place, time, period, state of, quality of, group of	-ure	state of being, process of, condition of, result of
-ic	having the characteristics of, causing	-ward	in the direction of
-ice	condition of, state of	-y	characterized by, inclined to, tending to
-ile	related to, capable of, suitable for		
-ion, -sion, -tion, -ation	act of, state of, process of		